学术英语写作研究

理论与方法

赵茵 张雯 李昂 著

清华大学出版社
北京

内 容 简 介

学术论文写作是获得学术进步的重要手段,而学术英语写作无疑是帮助研究人员表述个人学术成果的重要形式。

本书提供了进行规范性学术英语写作的理论与方法,在九个章节中,系统地阐述了如下内容:学术英语写作的价值与核心观点;学术英语语篇创作的过程,以及起草、修改和编辑的标准;较有代表性的学科领域中的学术英语语言、语篇以及语法的特色;图表等可视化信息的规范学术英语表达方法;如何设置学术英语写作中各部分内容的单元模块,以及各模块具体的写作方法等。

本书的目标读者,主要是以高质量学术英语写作为学习目的的学生或研究人员。对于学生来说,本书是进行学术英语写作的得力助手;对于研究人员来说,本书是提升学术英语写作水平的良好读物。

本书封面贴有清华大学出版社防伪标签,无标签者不得销售。
版权所有,侵权必究。举报:010-62782989,beiqinquan@tup.tsinghua.edu.cn。

图书在版编目(CIP)数据

学术英语写作研究:理论与方法 / 赵茵,张雯,李昂著. -- 北京:清华大学出版社,2025.5
ISBN 978-7-302-54094-6

Ⅰ.①学… Ⅱ.①赵…②张…③李… Ⅲ.①英语-写作-教学研究-高等学校 Ⅳ.H319.36

中国版本图书馆 CIP 数据核字 (2019) 第 241995 号

责任编辑:陈立静
装帧设计:杨玉兰
责任校对:张文青
责任印制:曹婉颖

出版发行:清华大学出版社
    网 址:https://www.tup.com.cn, https://www.wqxuetang.com
    地 址:北京清华大学学研大厦 A 座 邮 编:100084
    社 总 机:010-83470000 邮 购:010-62786544
    投稿与读者服务:010-62776969, c-service@tup.tsinghua.edu.cn
    质量反馈:010-62772015, zhiliang@tup.tsinghua.edu.cn
印 装 者:三河市铭诚印务有限公司
经 销:全国新华书店
开 本:185mm×260mm 印 张:8.25 字 数:286 千字
版 次:2025 年 5 月第 1 版 印 次:2025 年 5 月第 1 次印刷
定 价:49.80 元

产品编号:079159-01

PREFACE

There is nothing mysterious about academic writing. Typically, it provides an answer to a question (a solution to a problem) following a considered exploration of a subject. Relevant perspectives are introduced and analyzed in a systematic manner for composing academic writing. In academic research, while the result is important, it is the exploration which scores most of the marks. This is because a research result has little value if it is not obtained through a sound process. If you become skilled at being able to identify the key issues in relation to a particular problem, suggesting reasons and evidence in support of different perspectives, and completely making your own informed arguments, you will not only just be a good academic writer.

Who is this Book for

The identification of a structured and comprehensive account of the characteristics of a good academic essay and the skills needed to compose an essay are focuses of this book. This book has been written primarily for undergraduate/postgraduate students or researchers whose assessments will include academic essay writing. This book is inclusive of all disciplines by suggesting the skills and characteristics of academic writing which are commonly used across disciplines. Besides academic writing skills and characteristics, this book includes selection of content, creation of argument and composing method from integrated sources and so on. Students will find this book useful while producing academic writing. Academics can also benefit from it when setting and giving feedbacks on assignments.

How to Use this Book

The following is an overview of what will appear in each chapter.

● Chapter 1 (The Nature of Academic Writing) introduces the value of academic writing, characters of thesis statement and common features of academic writing.

● Chapter 2 (The Writing Process) introduces the essay invention process, the drafting, revising and editing criteria. The core of academic writing is the invention part. This chapter presents the possible ways of inventing a valuable idea.

● Chapter 3 (Linguistic Features of Academic Writing) explores the linguistic, discourse and grammatical features of academic writing of some representative disciplines.

• Chapter 4 (Academic Writing Style, Grammar, and Layout) provides advice about how to write in an academic manner. There is also advice about grammar and how to present essays.

• Chapter 5 (Critique and Synthesis Skills in Academic Writing) explains two very important skills in source literature reading and analyzing. Literature reading and analyzing is the fundamental step of academic writing, and the evaluation of the source materials calls for good critical and synthetic skills.

• Chapter 6 (Visual Skills in Academic Writing) introduces different approaches of presenting information visually. Academic writing involves greater chance of using tables, graphs, drawings and figures. Each has its own purpose and utility. So, it is significant to know when and where to use proper type of visual aids.

• Chapter 7 (Content in Academic Writing) tells discourse content unit options for each academic writing chapter. This chapter scopes the directions and perspectives of what need to cover in the writing of each chapter.

• Chapter 8 (Argument in Academic Writing) explains the importance of coherence in the design of argument in academic writing. In order to make the ideas clearly organized and explicitly articulated, some suggestions are given in this chapter.

• Chapter 9 (Composing Methods for Academic Writing) introduces systematically the specific methods used to compose each part of academic writing by offering examples and illustrations.

Throughout the book, the advice given is illustrated with examples. Not only will these examples help understand the advice, but also will be used as models for writing your own essays.

Academic writing — indeed all writing — is an art. No matter what to write, the ingenuity to solve many of the problems encountered is the essence of writing. Hope this book can solve some of your puzzles in academic writing and make your international academic communication more effective and rewarding. Sincere thanks to the scholars, teachers and my family who inspired, helped and encouraged me in the writing of this book. Suggestions and comments are always welcome. In the end, it is passion and integrity that made all the difference.

前言

学术论文写作是获得学术进步的重要手段之一。不论一项研究的结果多么令人惊叹,只有研究结果发表之后,这项学术研究才算完成。唯有如此,科学新知才能获得鉴定,并添加到现有的科学知识数据库中。

发现问题、提出方法、收集和分析数据、得出结论,把这样一个科学研究的过程付诸笔端,需要学习者和研究者专门学习并具备一套相对固定、成熟的思维习惯、语言规范及谋篇布局的理论和方法。学术研究是一种社会活动,它依赖于有效的交流。希望本书能促进学习者和研究者的有效学术交流。

目标读者

本书着力探寻学术写作的特点,以及学术写作者需要具备的技能和方法。本书的目标读者,主要是以高质量学术写作为学习目的和研究评价标准的学生或研究者。因为不同学科的学术研究目标和要求差异很大,甚至同一个学科的不同期刊要求也不同,所以不能给出一套普遍适用的建议。本书给出的是适用于大多数学科的基本原则和理论,还包含了内容选择、论述创新的理论和方法,以及文献综合分析与创作的原理及操作。对于学习者来说,本书是进行学术写作的得力助手;对于研究人员来说,本书是对写作进行反思的指导文献。

内容与章节设置

本书分为以下内容与章节。

- 第一章(The Nature of Academic Writing),介绍学术写作的价值、核心观点的特点,以及学术写作的共同特征。
- 第二章(The Writing Process),介绍学术语篇创作的过程,以及起草、修改和编辑的标准。创作是学术写作的灵魂。本章也探寻了可以激发创作并生成有价值观点的思维导图。
- 第三章(Linguistic Features of Academic Writing),探讨比较有代表性的学科领域中的学术语言、语篇以及语法的特色。
- 第四章(Academic Writing Style, Grammar, and Layout),提供如何进行规范性学术写作的建议,还包含了语法规则和写作规范。
- 第五章(Critique and Synthesis Skills in Academic Writing),解释在文献阅读、分析和筛选过程中非常重要的两个技能。文献阅读和分析是进行学术写作的基础,对于文献的评价和取舍,要求写作者具备良好的批判和综合能力。

● 第六章（Visual Skills in Academic Writing），介绍呈现可视化信息的不同方法。学术写作中会使用大量的图表等可视化信息来解释和表达观点，以期达到更有效的学术交流。每一种可视化信息的表达方式都有其特点和使用场合。本章对于何时何地用恰当方式进行可视化表达进行了分析。

● 第七章（Content in Academic Writing），讲述学术写作的每一个部分需要包含的内容单元模块，以及如何构建合理模块的方法。

● 第八章（Argument in Academic Writing），主要强调论述中逻辑和衔接的重要性，介绍了清晰的组织结构和明确表达的方法。

● 第九章（Composing Methods for Academic Writing），系统阐述学术写作中每一部分的写作方法，并使用真实案例进行具体分析。本章采用了大量的表格形式，为保持版式的连贯性，我们去掉了表头，特此说明。

全书介绍的理论和方法都有大量实例进行佐证。这些例子不仅可以帮助读者更加清晰地理解所介绍的方法，还可用作个人写作时的范例。

学术写作——实际上，所有的写作——都是一种艺术。无论要写什么，发现问题并解决问题的独创性才是学术写作的灵魂。希望本书能够解决一些学术写作中可能遇到的疑惑，使学生们或研究者们的国际学术交流更加有效、更有收获。

感谢在本书写作过程中鼓励和帮助过我们的学者及同事。由于水平有限，各种谬误或疏漏在所难免，敬请读者批评指正。

作　者

CONTENTS

Chapter 1 The Nature of Academic Writing 1
    1.1 Values of Academic Writing 2
    1.2 Thesis Statement of Academic Writing 2
    1.3 Common Features of Academic Writing 3

Chapter 2 The Writing Process 6
    2.1 Understanding the Task 6
    2.2 Gathering Data 8
    2.3 Invention 8
    2.4 Drafting 10
    2.5 Revision 13
    2.6 Editing 13

Chapter 3 Linguistic Features of Academic Writing 15
    3.1 Introduction 15
    3.2 Linguistic Features of Academic Writing 17

Chapter 4 Academic Writing Style, Grammar, and Layout 24
    4.1 Academic Writing Style 24
    4.2 Grammar 30
    4.3 Layout 31

Chapter 5 Critique and Synthesis Skills in Academic Writing 32
    5.1 Critical Reading 32
    5.2 What Is a Synthesis? 36
    5.3 Writing of Explanatory Synthesis 39
    5.4 Writing of Argument Synthesis 49

Chapter 6 Visual Skills in Academic Writing ... 41
6.1 Purpose of Using Visual Presentations ... 42
6.2 General Guidelines for Using Visual Presentations ... 44
6.3 Conclusion ... 46

Chapter 7 Content in Academic Writing ... 47
7.1 Role of Genre Knowledge ... 47
7.2 Discourse Content Unit Options for Each Dissertation Chapter ... 48
7.3 Strategies for Writing of Each Chapter ... 56
7.4 Suggestions on Selection of Content for Each Dissertation Chapter ... 57

Chapter 8 Argument in Academic Writing ... 66
8.1 Academic Writing Argument ... 66
8.2 Different Argument Structures of Academic Article Chapters ... 67

Chapter 9 Composing methods for academic writing ... 72
9.1 Thesis Introduction ... 73
9.2 Literature Review ... 81
9.3 Methodology ... 88
9.4 Results ... 99
9.5 Discussion of Results ... 108
9.6 Abstract ... 117

References ... 122

Chapter 1
The Nature of Academic Writing

Whatever program of study you are taking at university, at some point you will need to put words on paper or enter them in an electronic file. You might wish to make notes from a lecture you have attended, from a book chapter you have read, from a professional organization's website you have visited, or from an academic paper you have studied. And then there are assignments you need to complete. These might be essays, practical reports, PowerPoints, presentations, reviews of articles, webpages you are designing — the list could be long.

Each kind of communication you create has its own particular cluster of features. It is written for a particular audience with a certain purpose in mind. For example, in a social science or humanities discipline you might be asked to write an essay. In a science or engineering discipline, you might be required to submit a report on a laboratory investigation you'd just completed. In completing either writing task you would need to follow certain conventions. There are likely to be certain rules to follow about structure. You will normally be expected to adopt a certain kind of writing style, such as how informal or formal the writing is, the viewpoint you are writing, how citing and referencing will be used to underpin the argument in your writing, and so on.

A major challenge of academic writing is to write assignments in an appropriate academic style and with a suitable structure that develops an argument in an appropriate way. Unless you are taking a generic and introductory writing course, writing academically usually has a specific disciplinary context. Almost invariably you are writing for particular audience within a certain discipline and with a specific purpose in mind.

1.1 Values of Academic Writing

Given that academic writing is about developing your learning, and assessing your earning, academic writing normally consists of the following features.

- Reveal knowledge and understanding of the subject.
- Show the work is original.
- Follow the conventions of discipline, such as the document structure, writing style and viewpoint.
- Use scholarly methods: show accuracy and skill in investigating and discussing its subject; reveal the sources of information by citing and referencing; show evidence of critical analysis which includes considering the strengths and weaknesses of an argument and coming to conclusions about it.

Conventionally, most essays have a structure with a clear beginning (introduction), main body (development of an overall argument) and end (conclusion). This is based on the traditional notion of a lecture, which itself dates back to the conventions of the political debating chambers of ancient Greece and Rome: tell the audience what you are going to talk about, talk about it, and then tell them what you have talked about.

1.2 Thesis Statement of Academic Writing

Imagine you are writing an essay in humanities or social science, your tutor might ask you to express a clear opinion about the topic in your assignment. He or she might ask that you make this apparent in the introduction by making a thesis statement.

Commonly, a thesis statement is taken to be a sentence or two at the end of the introduction that summarizes a student's argument and point of view on the topic he is considering. For example, consider an essay assignment in economics and marketing about the topic "By reference to one or two large companies, and drawing upon appropriate economic or marketing theories, discuss strategies for making best use of the online environment in a business context." The thesis statement in its introduction might be: "Given that the World Wide Web offers large companies huge potential for marketing and promotion, businesses should make best use of it, by taking every opportunity to target their advertising to specific potential customers while at the same time offering strong support online to existing customers."

Being asked to include a thesis statement can make for "stronger" writing, insofar as you are writing to defend the argument. In doing so, you still need to consider both sides of the argument — evidence and reasoning both for and against the position you have chosen to take. However, in some disciplines the use of thesis statement is not encouraged. Conclusions are not expected to be given away at the beginning. This approach—not having a thesis statement—is common in scientific and engineering disciplines.

1.3 Common Features of Academic Writing

The following features apply to many kinds of academic writing.

- Being written for a narrow range of purposes, to develop or assess learning.
- Depending on its purpose, academic writing has particular requirements in terms of structure, organization, and presentation.
- Presenting a structured argument overall, supported by secondary arguments.
- Building up arguments from evidence and reasoning, either your own or from what you have read, heard or observed.
- Adopting an appropriate writing style, usually in formal written English.
- Following the conventions of a particular discipline, using appropriate technical vocabulary and agreed principles for citing and referencing.

1.3.1 Academic Writing as Argument

Academic writing is almost always about argument. Description is important, but usually it is a starting point to build an argument, or part of an argument. Thinking of your writing as argument encourages you to weave facts, ideas or opinions into a reasoned overall account. Academic writing needs to go beyond mere description to critical analysis.

Different disciplines regard as suitable evidence and reasoning can vary, and different assignments within the same discipline might require different forms of evidence. For example, in a psychology course, an individual's own experience of being a pupil at school might be appropriate evidence to include in an essay about models of behavioral psychology applied to classroom practice. Another research, setting a psychology literature review in which there is an emphasis on quantitative research (analysis of numerical data), might not regard personal experience as suitable evidence. An overall argument contains the following features.

- The author gives evidence and reasoning, assembled as reasons (sometimes called supporting arguments, premises or propositions) that support the eventual conclusion.
- Reasons are presented in a logical order, and an overall line of reasoning, takes the reader convincingly through to the conclusion.
- There is a conclusion—the position that the author wants the reader to accept.

- In short, an academic argument contains evidence and reasoning that guide the reader, through an overall line of reasoning to a conclusion.

1.3.2 Being Critical

Being critical involves evaluating what you read, or in other words, making judgements about how relevant and important it is in relation to your task. Being critical does not just involve being negative about what you have read. It involves weighing up both sides — the pluses and minuses — of what you have read, seen or heard, and then drawing your own conclusion as to its value in relation to your assignment, or to your learning overall. In this sense, the flaws or weakness in one reasoning should be noticed by assessors who will help guide you in more fruitful directions. By thinking for yourself, and helped by others' questioning, higher-level skills are encouraged to be developed, including the following.

- **Analyzing.** Reading the work of others and breaking down their arguments into component parts in order to better understand them.
- **Synthesizing.** Building your own arguments, drawing upon the work of others.
- **Applying.** Taking facts or ideas and using them in another context, such as a practical, real-world one.
- **Evaluating.** Judging the validity of elements of an argument, whether your own or those of others.

1.3.3 Being Formal

The writing as an argument is usually much more formal. It normally needs to meet the following requirements.

- Employing words that have precise meaning For example, emplay "analyze" rather than "think about".
- Avoiding jargon or colloquial English.
- Not using contractions. Instead of "can't" and "doesn't", write "cannot" and "does not".
- On many occasions one avoids writing in the personal voice (you, I or we). Instead, the impersonal voice is often encouraged. For example write, "The analysis was carried out" rather than "We carried out the analysis".
- Academic writing usually avoids using direct or rhetorical questions: for example, "Was the solution to the problem within the hands of the protesters?"

1.3.4 Using Words with Precision

Academic writing often goes beyond description. It usually involves being critical and making judgements about the value of sources of information that are used in writing an assignment. In academic writing, words tend to be used with greater precision than in everyday writing.

The words in Table 1.1 might be used in academic writing. Each verb has a specific meaning.

Table 1.1 Verbs in Acedemic Writing

Verb	Meaning
Compare	Point out similarities and differences between two views or amorg more views. This might involve coming to a conclusion as to the preferred view.
Contrast	Set two views in opposition in order to highlight the differences between them.
Evalute	Assess the value of something, which might include offering a personal opinion.
Interpret	Make clear the meaning of something. This might include giving a personal judgment.
Justify	Give reasons for decisions or conclusions reached, which might include responding to possible objections.
Outline	Give an overview of the general principles and/or main features of a subject, omitting fine details.

During a lecture, a member of staff might use the phrase "now, let's look at..." to mean "now let's consider..." rather than "now let us observe..." Using "look at" (when it does not mean "observe") is perfectly acceptable in speech. In academic writing, however, the use of the phrase "look at" can be replaced by more specific verbs that are more precise in their meaning.

Chapter 2
The Writing Process

The process of academic writing can be divided into stages. Writers sometimes can then turn the overwhelming task of writing a paper into manageable pieces that collectively build to a final draft. Generally, the stages of academic writing can be summarized in Table 2.1 and Figure 2.1 (Carmel, Huang, & Tam, 2007, pp. 17~18).

The writing process flows from left to right, but it is not one-way. It is a recursive process; that is, the process tends to loop back on itself. It is impossible to follow a straight-line path to the end. Writing is messier than that. For example, once you draft your ideas in an outline form, you may see gaps in the information you've collected, requiring you to circle back and gather more data before proceeding to the next step. The circling can happen at any point. Perhaps you are writing a draft and your ideas take you in an unexpected direction. You stop to consider: Do I want to follow this through? If so, you will need to rethink the overall organization of your work. You move forward as you write to a finished product. But moving forward is seldom a straight-line process.

2.1 Understanding the Task

To be sure that you are fulfilling the requirements for a writing task, some of the key items needed to know are the *purpose*, *scope* and *audience* for your task. "Purpose" concerns why you have been given the task. "Scope" concerns the detail and width of the task. "Audience" is the assumed reader of the assignment or the writing. Consider the tasks, for example, as the samplings of topics that have been assigned in a broad range of undergraduate courses:

Table 2.1 The stages of Academic writing

Understanding the task	Gathefinil data	Invention	Drafting	Revision	Editing
Read orcreate the assignment. Understand scope and audience.	Locate and review information and formulate an approach.	Use various techniques to generate a tentative statement of the direction you intend to pursue.	Sketch the paper you intend to write. You will expect to discover and invent a new plan as you write.	Revise at the global level, reshaping or rearranging. Revise at the local level, ensuring that each paragraph is well reasoned.	Revise at the sentence level of style and brevity. Revise for correctness, grammar, punctuation, usage, and spelling.

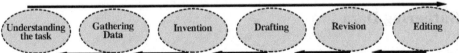

Figure 2.1 The stages of Academic writing

Art history. Discuss the main differences between Romanesque and Gothic sculpture, using the sculptures of Jeremiah (St. Pierre Cathedral) and St. Theodore (Chartres Cathedral) as major examples.

Physics. Research and write a paper on solar cell technology, covering the following areas which are basic physical theory, history and development, structure and materials, types and characteristics, practical uses, state of the art, and future prospects.

Political Science. Explain the contours of California's water policy in the past few decades and then, by focusing on one specific controversy, explain and analyze the way in which this policy was adapted and why.

Sociology. Write on one of the following topics. (1) A critical comparison of two or more theories of deviance. (2) A field or library research study of those in a specific deviant career. (3) Portrayals of deviance in popular culture. (4) Old age as a form of deviance in the context of youth culture. (5) The relationship between homelessness and mental illness.

Some of these papers allow students a considerable range of choice (within the general subject); others are highly specific in requiring students to address a particular issue. As with all academic writing, your first task is to make sure you understand the assignment. One useful technique for doing so is to locate the assignment's key verb(s), which will stipulate exactly what is expected.

The directive words of essay questions are in Table 2.2 (Moss & Holder, 1988, pp. 17~18). When you are asked to *criticize* the present electoral system, you are not answering the question if you merely *explain* how it operates. A paper is satisfactory only if it answers directly the question that was asked.

Table 2.2 The Directive Words of Essay Qaestions

summarize	sum up; give the main point briefly
evaluate	talk over the advantages and limitations
contrast	bring out the points of difference
explain	make clear, interpret
describe	give a word picture of
compare	bring out similarity and difference
discuss	consider from various point of view

justify	show good reason
illustrate	use a word picture, a diagram, a chart, or example to clarify a point

In addition to understanding the major task of the assignment, the length of writing and the research method are also important for deciding how to compose your assignment. But above all, if possible, please choose the topic you have interests in. Motivational theory suggests that an intrinsically motivating task will result in an easier and better performance (Ryan & Deci, 2000).

2.2 Gathering Data

2.2.1 Literature Search

There are different ways to collect data, such as getting guidance from books, viewing key papers, and attending relevant lectures. Those sources can provide leads to further sources, such as in the reference lists at the end of a book or an article. Web search engines such as Google Scholar or literature databases such as Web of Science can be used. More recent articles that have referred to earlier key papers can be discovered. Those ways of gathering data can help reveal curiosity and independence of mind.

It is helpful to read with a clear purpose in mind when studying an article, book chapter or reputable website. Strategical reading helps to hunt for what is needed to complete the task. It works on the well-established principle that reading a piece of work two or three times, with specific purpose in mind, is usually much more effective than reading through a source document slowly from beginning to end only once.

2.2.2 Types of Data

Primary data. Primary data refer to the data gathered directly by a researcher by using the research methods appropriate to particular field of study, such as experiments or observations in the sciences, surveys or interviews in the social sciences. Primary data can be divided into two categories: quantitative data and qualitative data. Generally, quantitative data encompasse issues of "how many" or "how often", while qualitative data account for such issues as "what kind" and "why".

Secondary data. Secondary data are used in undergraduate assignments. Secondary data may refer to information and ideas collected or generated by others who have performed their own primary and/or secondary research. The data gathered for most undergraduate academic writing will consist of library research and online database and resources.

2.3 Invention

Regardless of the name, invention is an important part of the process that typically overlaps with data gathering. The preliminary data you gather on a topic will inform the choices you make in defining your project. As you invent, you will often return to gather more data. Writers sometimes skip the invention stage, preferring to save time by launching directly from data gathering into writing a draft. But many efforts go wrong when writers choose on extremely broad or narrow topic.

2.3.1 Choosing and Narrowing the Topic

Suppose you have been assigned an open-ended, ten-page paper in an introductory course on environmental science. Not only do you have to choose a subject, but you also have to narrow down it sufficiently and formulate your thesis. Usually materials from books or book chapters, journal articles, lectures or online databases are the fundamental sources for generating and narrowing the idea. Having read several sources on energy conservation and having decided that you'd like to use them, you might limit the topic by asking about the aspects, and deciding to focus on energy conservation which relates to motor vehicles. "Energy-efficient vehicles" offers more specific focus than "energy conservation" does. Still, the revised focus is too broad. So with more references to the reference materials, some notes may be jotted down as follows.

- Types of energy-efficient vehicles
  All-electric vehicles
  Hybrid vehicles
  Fuel-cell vehicles
- Government action to encourage development of energy-efficient vehicles
  Additional taxes imposed on high-mileage vehicles
  Subsidies to developers of energy-efficient vehicles

In general, you will have to spend enough time gathering data, brainstorming, gathering more data, and then brainstorming again in order to limit your subject before attempting to write about it. Assume that the final settled topic which is appropriate for a ten-page paper is as follows:

Encourage the development of fuel cell vehicles

The process of choosing an initial subject depends heavily on the reading one does. The more one reads, the deeper the understandingis. The deeper the understandingis, the likelier the topic will be developed from a broad one to a manageable one. In the example above, reading ranges narrowly from the "energy-efficient vehicles" to "fuel cell vehicles". In this way, reading stimulates you to decide an appropriate topic for your paper. Your process here can go around from stage 1 to stage 2 of the process, each movement bringing you closer to establishing a clear focus before you attempt to write your paper.

2.3.2 Invention Strategies

Writers use a number of strategies for thinking through ideas in writing. Several strategies are provided below.

FREEWRITING

As a first step in the invention stage, you might sit down with an assignment and writing continuously. If you stick with it and try to let yourself write spontaneously, you will be surprised at what comes out. You might generate logical connections between ideas that you haven't noticed before. As a second step, you might take that idea and free write about it, shift to a different invention strategy to explore one idea, or even to begin to draft a thesis, depending on the extent to which your idea is well formed.

LISTING

Some writers find it helpful to make lists of their ideas, breaking significant ideas into sub lists and seeing where they lead. Create lists by putting related ideas out of the notes or the readings. So, list ideas as a way of brainstorming, and generate another list for the structure of the draft.

CLUSTERING AND BRANCHING

Clustering involves writing an idea in the middle of a page and circling it. Then draw lines leading from that circle to new circles in which you write subtopics of that central idea. Pick the subtopics that interest you most, and draw lines leading to more circles wherein you note important aspects of the subtopics (see figare. 2.2). Branching follows the same principle, but instead of placing ideas in circles, write them on lines that branch off to other lines.

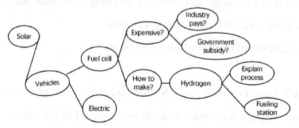

Figure 2.2　Subtopics of a Central Idea

Clustering and branching is a useful begianing in invention, for it helps isolate the topics about which you are most knowledgeable. As you branch off into the subtopics of a main paper topic, the number of ideas you generate in relation to these topics will help show where you have the most knowledge and interest.

2.4 Drafting

It is usually best to begin drafting a paper after you have decided on a working or manageable thesis. While consulting the results of your efforts during invention, you have a number of steps to proceed with drafting the paper.

2.4.1 Writing a Thesis Statement

A thesis statement is a one-sentence summary of a paper's content. It is similar, actually, to a paper's conclusion, but it lacks the conclusion's concern for broad implications and significance. For a writer in the drafting stages, the thesis statement establishes a focus, a basis on which to include or exclude information. For the reader of a finished product, the thesis anticipates the author's discussion. A thesis, therefore, is an essential tool for both writers and readers of academic paper.

THE COMPONENTS OF A THESIS

What distinguishes a thesis from any other sentence is that the thesis presents the controlling idea of the paper. The subject of a thesis, and the assertion about it, must present the right balance between the general and the specific to allow discussion. The discussion might include definitions, details, comparisons and contrasts.

When writing thesis statements, remember that the more general your subjectis and the more complex the assertionis, the longer the paper will be. To write an effective thesis and thus a controlled, effective paper, the subject and claims about it should be limited. A manageable topic will be achieved by narrowing process. A topic will be converted to an assertion or a claim about it which will be explained and supported in the paper.

MAKING AN ASSERTION

After reading and gathering information, and brainstorming ideas about the assignment, a writer will be knowledgeable enough to have something to say with a base of a combination of his/her own thinking.

If you have trouble making an assertion, devote more time to invention strategies. Try writing the subject and then listing everything you know and feel. And from the list, you will discover an assertion which can be used to fashion a working thesis. Make several assertions about the topic in order to pursue related discussions, as is in the following.

(1) Fuel cell technology has emerged as a promising approach to developing energy-efficient vehicles.

(2) To reduce our dependence on nonrenewable fossil fuel, the federal government should encourage the development of fuel cell vehicles.

These working theses are hypotheses to be tested. The working thesis is subject to constant adjustments in order to pursue related discussions.

PLANNING A STRUCTURE

A working thesis will help sketch the structure. The following is the third thesis on the fuel cell technology.

(3) The federal government should subsidize the development of fuel cell vehicles as well as the hydrogen infrastructure needed to support them; otherwise, the economy will be increasingly

vulnerable to recession and the dependence on the continued flow of foreign oil.

If a paper based on this thesis structure is to be well developed, the writer must commit himself or herself to explaining the following questioas. (1) why fuel cell vehicles are a preferred alternative to gasoline-powered vehicles? (2) why fuel cell vehicles require a hydrogen infrastructure? (3) why the government needs to subsidize industry in developing fuel cell vehicles? (4) how continued reliance on fossil fuel technology? This thesis therefore helps the writer plan the paper, which should include a section on each of these four topics.

2.4.2 Writing Introductions and Conclusions

INTRODUCTIONS

The purpose of an introduction is to prepare the reader to enter the world of the paper. The introduction makes the connection between the more familiar world inhabited to the reader and the less familiar world of the writer's particular topic. There are many ways for opening a paper like historical review, working from the general to the specific, and from the specific to the general, posing a question, and directly stating the thesis.

The following is an introduction to a paper on effect of teacher motivation (Moskovsky, Alrabai, Paolini, & Ratcheva, 2013).

The study of second language (SL) acquisition has in the past 40 years been among the most dynamic and rapidly expanding sciences within the humanities. Few issues have been seen as much attention by SL researchers as the role that motivation plays with regard to the attainment of non-primary languages. In a field that is notorious for its lack of agreement on almost anything, there is essentially a consensus that SL motivation is related to achievement and that SL motivation is the driving force that enables learners to expend the continuously sustained effort language learning requires. It is widely accepted that, everything else being equal, more motivated learners would be more successful at learning the second/foreign language than less motivated learners, and that without sufficient motivation even highly competent and cognitively capable individuals may be unable to accomplish long-term goals (DÖrnyei & Csize´r, 1998; Wlodkowski, 1999; Cheng & Do □rnyei, 2007; Guilloteaux & Do □rnyei, 2008). It has also been suggested that motivation influences ... has the potential to determine to what extent these factors are realized (Gardner, 2001; Oxford & Shearin, 1994, among others)... Levels of motivation have been found to vary, sometimes substantially, among individual learners, as well as among groups of learners (Guilloteaux, 2007, among many others)....

The quotations by DÖrnyei & Csize´r etc. help set the stage for the discussion of democracy by presenting the reader with provocative remarks. Later, the quotations by Gardner and Guilloteaux etc. prepares the theme of change that will be central to the paper as a whole. Quoting the words of others offers many points to begin your paper. You can agree with the quotation. You can expand.

You can sharply disagree. You can use the quotation to set a context.

CONCLUSIONS

A conclusion is the part of your paper in which you restate and expand on your thesis. The simplest conclusion is a summary of the paper. But depending on the needs of writing, a summary might be followed by a discussion of the paper's significance or its implications for future study. The conclusions of better papers often reveal authors who want to connect their concerns with the broader concerns of society.

Two points need to be noted. First, no matter how clever or beautifully executed, a conclusion cannot be the remedy for a poorly written paper. Second, the conclusion carries rhetorical weight. Rhetoric and drama in a conclusion are fine as long as they do not violate the balance of the paper.

2.5 Revision

The word revision can be used to describe all modifications one makes to a written document. However, it is useful to distinguish among three kinds of revision (Carmel et al., 2007, p. 58)

Global revisions focus on the thesis, the type and pattern of evidence employed, the overall organization, the match between thesis and content, and the tone. A global revision may also emerge from a change in purpose.

Local revisions focus on paragraphs, for example, topic and transitional sentences, the type of evidence presented within a paragraph, evidence added, modified, or dropped within a paragraph, and logical connections from one sentence to another within a paragraph.

A good paper needs to follow the principles of *unity, coherence,* and *development*(Ding, Wu, Zhong, & Guo, 2009, pp. 64~67).

Unity means that a paper is unified when focused on a main point. Thus, the first step for determining unity is to examine your introduction and make sure you have a clear thesis. Next, check your paper's paragraphs to make sure your points are related to that thesis.

Coherence means logical interconnectedness. When things cohere, separate elements hold together and make a whole. All subordinate points addressed in the body of the paper clearly relate to the main point expressed in the thesis.

Development says that good papers are also well developed, meaning that their points are fully explained and supported. Sufficient support for the arguments is provided by using examples, the opinions of authorities on the subject, and sound logic to hold together.

2.6 Editing

Grammar and punctuation is the target of the editing step. Grammar and punctuation follows more widely accepted, objective standards. It has conventions, or rules that people working in academic, professional, and business environments adopt as a standard of communication. Rules are easily found in up-to-date writing handbooks. Common sentence-level errors are listed below in Table 2.3.

Table 2.3 Common Sentence-level Errors

Errors in Grammar
Sentence fragments — incomplete sentences missing a subject or predicate
Run-on sentences — two independent clauses joined together without the proper conjunctions
Comma splices — two independent clauses joined with only a comma
subject-verb agreement errors — the verb doesn't match the plural or singular nature of the subject
Pronoun usage — pronoun reference errors, lack of clear pronoun reference
Errors in Punctuation
Misplaced commas, missing commas, improper use of semicolons or colons, missing apostrophes, and the like
Errors in Spelling
Misspelled words

Chapter 3
Linguistic Features of Academic Writing

3.1 Introduction

Many speakers of English share the view that the language of academic writing is peculiar, not only different from everyday speech, but also different from most other registers of English. A common stereotype of academic prose is that it is deliberately complex, and more concerned with impressing readers than communicating ideas—all making it needlessly difficult to understand.

The primary focus of these negative attitudes is on the use of rare and obscure words and phrases. The perception is that these words are often chosen to impress readers rather than efficiently convey new information.

These stereotypes about writing in humanities writing continue right up to the present. For example, Pinker (2014) discussed the question of "Why academics stink at writing", and notes the following.

> *The most popular answer outside the academy is the cynical one: [...] Scholars in the softer fields spout obscure verbiage to hide the fact that they have nothing to say. They dress up the trivial and obvious with the trappings of scientific sophistication, hoping to bamboozle their audiences with highfalutin gobbledygook.*

Texts that seem to illustrate this prose style are not hard to find. For example, the journal *Philosophy and Literature* (Hagberg) sponsored a "Bad Writing Contest" from 1995 to 1998, which celebrated "the most stylistically lamentable passages found in scholarly books and articles published in the last few years." The winner of the 1998 contest was Judith Butler, "a

Guggenheim Fellowship-winning professor of rhetoric and comparative literature at the University of California at Berkeley". The first-prize sentence, singled out for its "anxiety-inducing obscurity", reads as follows (Sample Text 1).

The move from a structuralist account in which capital is understood to structure social relations in relatively homologous ways to a view of hegemony in which power relations are subject to repetition, convergence, and rearticulation brought the question of temporality into the thinking of structure, and marked a shift from a form of Althusserian theory that takes structural totalities as theoretical objects to one in which the insights into the contingent possibility of structure inaugurate a renewed conception of hegemony as bound up with the contingent sites and strategies of the rearticulation of power.

Judith Butler. 1997.
Further Reflections on the Conversations of Our Time
Diacritics, 27(1): 13~15.

Pinker describes the primary goal of humanities writing as "self-presentation" rather than the communication of information. This goal results in a "self-conscious style", where the author's primary concern is "to escape being convicted of philosophical naïveté about his own enterprise". In contrast, science research writing is associated with a "classic style" focused on the communication of information. (Pinker, 2014)

The linguistic characteristics of science writing are dramatically different from the "self-conscious" style of humanities writing. Science articles can be boring, relying on simple syntactic constructions, as is in the following example (Sample Text 2).

The neurites are black on a yellow-brown background in the original preparation (see Figure 5). One neurite can be traced coursing through the basement membrane of the epidermis (arrow). The neurites appear to penetrate the cytoplasm of the epidermal cells (see also Fig. 11).

Bryce L. Munger. 1965.
The Intraepidermal Innervation of the Snout Skin of the Opossum
Journal of Cell Biology, 26(1): 79~97.

Although there are often technical terms in this style, those terms usually refer to physical entities rather than abstract concepts. The overall stylistic effect is to emphasize the direct communication of information.

Our goals in this chapter are not to enter into the debate about "good" and "bad" academic writing. But the goal of this chapter is to investigate the linguistic characteristics of academic writing, including the differences between humanities writing and science writing.

In the next section, we provide more detailed discussion of the grammatical features associated with academic writing, and the striking grammatical differences between humanities and science writing.

3.2 Linguistic Features of Academic Writing

3.2.1 Obscurity of Academic Writing

Researchers in the humanities would argue that they do not simply document human experiences that are familiar to us all; rather, they are constantly offering new interpretations of those experiences, and they do so in highly technical ways that are not easily understood by the non-expert. For example, consider the following excerpt from a literary criticism article (Sample Text 3).

Published in the wake of the Great Exhibition of 1851, it maps out the contours of interiority in a world newly captivated by the peculiar resonance of things. Though Bronte liked to think that her novel "touched on no matter of public interest," its conception of the psychological interior was significantly inflected by its setting in mid-century Thing City (Letters 3: 75). Villette places interiority in an intimate connection with object-filled interiors even as it hopes for an inner life that eludes the varied fetishisms of Thing City. This nostalgia for a more pristine and private form of psychological depth is, in turn, articulated in terms that reveal how entrenched persons are in the public empire of things. Villette constitutes an attempt to negotiate between a critique of commodity fetishism and a paradoxically fetishistic preoccupation with the traces and tokens of inner life. The novel suggests that the bourgeois subject, though it comes into being through its relations with things, is defined by the nostalgic notion that its true interiority has been lost under the pressure of things.

Eva Badowska. 2005
Charlotte: Brontë's "Villette" and the Art of Bourgeois Interiority
PMLA, 120: 1509~1523

One of the most salient characteristics of this text is the highly specialized vocabulary. Abstract technical terms are common in this passage, such as *interiority* and *fetishisms*. In addition, relatively common words like *objects, contours, interior, depth,* and *life* are used together with technical terms to produce complex phrases referring to highly abstract concepts, such as *the peculiar resonance of things, object-filled interiors, the contours of interiority, nostalgia for a more pristine and private form of psychological depth, the public empire of things, and a paradoxically fetishistic preoccupation with the traces and tokens of inner life.* Taken together, these abstract terms and complex phrases make it difficult for the non-specialist reader to understand the content of the literary analysis presented in the article.

Research writing in the sciences is probably even more difficult for the non-expert to understand. The general goal of science research is to discover new information about the natural world, identifying new phenomena and explaining previously identified phenomena and patterns. Scientists require new words to refer to these previously undocumented phenomena and processes, resulting in articles that can be almost unreadable to the non-experts. The following passage from a biochemistry research article is a illustration. (Sample Text 4).

Several kinases phosphorylate vimentin, the most common intermediate filament protein, in mitosis. Aurora-B and Rho-kinase regulate vimentin filament separation through the cleavage furrow-specific vimentin phosphorylation. Cdk1 also phosphorylates vimentin from prometaphase to metaphase, but its significance has remained unknown. Here we demonstrated a direct interaction between Plk1 and vimentin-Ser55 phosphorylated by Cdk1, an event that led to Plk1 activation and further vimentin phosphorylation. Plk1 induced the phosphorylation of vimentin-Ser82, which was elevated from metaphase and maintained until the end of mitosis. This elevation followed the Cdk1-induced vimentin-Ser55 phosphorylation and was impaired by Plk1 depletion.

T. Yamaguchi et al. 2005.
Phosphorylation by Cdk1 induces Plk1-mediated vimentin phosphorylation during mitosis
Journal of Cell Biology, 171(3): 431~436.

Most readers of the present book have never encountered the verb to *phosphorylate*, or nouns like *kinases, vimentin, prometaphase, metaphase,* and *phosphorylation.* Since we have no idea what these terms refer to, the entire passage means little to us. Thus, the vocabulary of science research writing is similarly technical to the vocabulary of humanities prose, supporting the stereotype that all academic writing is complex and hard to understand.

It is much more difficult to notice the typical grammatical structures used in these academic texts. However, when considering at the grammatical level, we discover that there are important linguistic differences among the various disciplines of academic writing; and in particular, the language of science research writing is quite different from the language of humanities prose.

3.2.2 Linguistic Features in Academic Writing of Different Disciplines SIMILARITY

There are actually many ways in which academic texts differ from one another. For example, we discussed in previous sections how humanities research writing differs in its goals and topics from science research writing. Despite those differences, all academic written texts can seem similar linguistically. For example, both the following texts rely on specialized technical vocabulary, including many nominalizations.

Literary criticism text

exhibition, interiority, resonance, conception, connection, fetishisms, preoccupation, relations

Biochemistry text

separation, cleavage, phosphorylation, significance, interaction, activation, ability, elevation, depletion

The two texts both use some specialized grammatical features, which are somehow peculiar and difficult to understand. For example, passive voice — a grammatical feature often associated with academic prose — is commonly used in both of the following texts.

Literary criticism text

a world newly captivated by... things

its conception... was significantly inflected by its setting

this nostalgia... is, in turn, articulated...

the bourgeois subject... is defined by the nostalgic notion that its true interiority has been lost

Biochemistry text

vimentin-Ser55 phosphorylated by Cdk1

the phosphorylation of vimentin-Ser82 ... was elevated from metaphase and maintained until the end of mitosis

This elevation... was impaired by Plk1 depletion

DIFFERENCES

1) Attributive Adjectives

However, a more careful analysis uncovers ways in which the above two texts differ in their linguistic characteristics. For example, attributive adjectives are very common in humanities academic writing.

Literary criticism text

Great Exhibition, peculiar resonance, public interests, psychological interior, intimate connection, inner life, varied fetishisms, a more pristine and private form of psychological depth, public empire, a paradoxically fetishistic preoccupation, nostalgic notion

Attributive adjectives are generally less common in science research writing, and the biochemistry text is typical in this regard, with only two examples.

direct interaction

further vimentin phosphorylation.

2) Noun Pre-modifier

However, science writing tends to employ nouns as pre-modifiers to modify a head noun.

Biochemistry text

filament protein, vimentin filament separation, the cleavage furrow-specific vimentin, phosphorylation Plk1 activation, vimentin phosphorylation

In contrast, pre-modifying nouns are much less common in humanities writing, as is illustrated by the literary criticism text, which employs only two occurrences.

Literary criticism text

Thing City, commodity fetishism

3) Appositive Noun Phrase

Further consideration of biochemistry text illustrates an additional grammatical device that is much more common in science writing than humanities writing: appositive noun phrases. The following are noun phrases that modify the immediately preceding head noun.

Biochemistry text

vimentin, the most common intermediate filament protein

a direct interaction between Plk1 and vimentin-Ser55 phosphorylated by Cdk1, an event that led to Plk1 activation and further vimentin

4) Density of Verbs

The literary criticism text utilizes three or four verbs in each sentence, while the biochemistry text uses only one or two verbs per sentence.

Literary criticism text: Verbs marked in bold

***Published** in the wake of the Great Exhibition of 1851, it **maps** out the contours of interiority in a world newly **captivated** by the peculiar resonance of things. Though Bronte **liked** to **think** that her novel "**touche[d]** on no matter of public interest," its conception of the psychological interior **was** significantly **inflected** by its setting in mid-century Thing City (Letters 3: 75). Villette **places** interiority in an intimate connection with object-filled interiors even as it **hopes** for an inner life that **eludes** the varied fetishisms of Thing City. This nostalgia for a more pristine and private form of psychological depth **is**, in turn, **articulated** in terms that **reveal** how **entrenched** persons **are** in the public empire of things. Villette **constitutes** an attempt to **negotiate** between a critique of commodity fetishism and a paradoxically fetishistic preoccupation with the traces and tokens of inner life. The novel **suggests** that the bourgeois subject, though it **comes** into being through its relations with* things, **is defined** by the nostalgic notion that its true interiority **has been lost** under the pressure of things.

Biochemistry text: Verbs marked in bold

*Several kinases **phosphorylate** vimentin, the most common intermediate filament protein, in mitosis. Aurora-B and Rho-kinase **regulate** vimentin filament separation through the cleavage furrow-specific vimentin phosphorylation. Cdkl also **phosphorylates** vimentin from prometaphase to metaphase, but its significance **has remained** unknown. Here we **demonstrated** a direct interaction between Plk1 and vimentin-Ser55 **phosphorylated** by Cdkl, an event that **led** to Plk1 activation and further vimentin phosphorylation. Plk1 **induced** the phosphorylation of vimentin-Ser82, which **was elevated** from metaphase and **maintained** until the end of mitosis. This elevation **followed** the Cdkl-induced vimentin-Ser55 phosphorylation and **was impaired** by Plk1 depletion.*

It turns out that this difference in the density of verbs reflects that a biochemistry text employs very simple syntactic structures, with few embedded dependent clauses, while the literary criticism text is characterized by a high density of dependent clauses. These two texts, which are typical of their respective disciplines, illustrate that there are systemically grammatical differences in the research writing amorg different academic disciplines. When compared to conversation or popular written registers (like fiction or newspaper report), it makes sense to treat academic writing as a general register with distinctive grammatical characteristics. At the same time, though, there are systematic patterns of linguistic variation that distinguish the different types of academic writing. These differences are related to other two stereotypes about academic writing: the beliefs that academic prose employs complex and elaborated grammar, and that it is maximally explicit in meaning.

3.2.3 Academic Writing: Complex Grammar and Explicit Meanings

Discussions in the last section contribute to the general perception that academic writing is more complex, structurally elaborated, and explicit in meaning than most other spoken and written registers. Hughes (1996, pp. 33~34) notes these characteristics, writing that spoken grammar employs "simple and short clauses, with little elaborate embedding", in contrast to written discourse, which employs "longer and more complex clauses with embedded phrases and clauses", "explicit and varied marking of clause relations", "explicit presentation of ideas", and "explicit indication of text organization".

In descriptive linguistics, grammatical complexity and structural elaboration is strongly associated with the use of dependent clauses. By definition, a "simple" clause has only a subject, verb, and object or complement. A "simple" noun phrase has a determiner and head noun. Additions or modifications to these patterns result in "complex" and "elaborated" grammar. In particular, linguists have traditionally singled out dependent clauses as the most important type of grammatical complexity and structural elaboration (Carter & McCarthy, 2006, p. 489; Huddleston, 1984, p. 378; Purpura, 2004, p. 91; Willis, 2003, p. 192).

The measurement of grammatical complexity can be done in terms of the T-unit: a main clause and all associated dependent clauses. Wolfe-Quintero, Inagaki, and Kim (1998, pp. 118~119) recommend variables like the number of dependent clauses per T-unit as the "best [...] complexity measures so far", and numerous researchers in applied linguistics have applied similar measures in their research (Brown, Iwashita, & McNamara, 2005; Ellis & Yuan, 2004; Larsen-Freeman, 2006; Li, 2000; Nelson & Van Meter, 2007; Norrby & Hakansson, 2007).

Of course, multiple embedded clauses do result in discourse that is more complex than alternative styles that rely on simple clauses, all other things being equal. And some written academic texts illustrate this type of grammatical complexity. For example, the literary criticism text discussed in the last section provides a good example of academic writing that employs extensive use of dependent clauses. In fact, all sentences in that passage incorporate multiple dependent clauses, often with multiple levels of embedding. Here we can see a verb complement clause, an adverbial clause, and a noun complement clause.

The novel **suggests**
    [that the bourgeois subject,
        *[though it **comes** into being through its relations with things],*
            ***is defined** by the nostalgic notion*
                *[that its true interiority **has been lost** under the*
                      pressure of things]

However, there is not only one type of grammatical complexity — associated with clausal embedding. Consider the first two sentences from Sample Text 4. Both the following sentences have a simple clause structure with only a single main verb and no embedded dependent clauses.

1. Several kinases **phosphorylate** vimentin, the most common intermediate filament protein, in mitosis.

2. Aurora-B and Rho-kinase **regulate** vimentin filament separation through cleavage furrow-specific vimentin phosphorylation.

However, even though there are no dependent clauses, these sentences convey much embedded information. That information is expressed in embedded phrases rather than dependent clauses. However, the same information could be conveyed more explicitly through the use of multiple clauses. Thus compare 1b and 2b to the original sentences 1 and 2.

*1b. Vimentin **is** the most common intermediate filament protein; these proteins **are structured to form** intermediate filaments; kinases **phosphorylate** vimentin; this process **occurs** during the process of mitosis.*

*2b. Vimentin filament can be separated; Aurora-B and Rho-kinase regulate that separation; **the separation occurs when** something phosphorylates vimentin specifically **where a furrow** begins the process of **creating cleavage***

Sample Text 4 above illustrates a grammatical discourse style where information is conveyed through phrasal devices rather than through the use of dependent clauses. These phrasal features include nouns as a pre-modifier of another noun (e.g. filament protein, vimentin filament separation, and cleavage furrow-specific vimentin phosphorylation), appositive noun phrases (e.g. vimentin, the most common intermediate filament protein), and prepositional phrases (e.g. in mitosis, through [...] phosphorylation). These devices constitute a second major type of grammatical complexity.

Is academic writing explicit in the expression of meaning in this way? It turns out that the complexity devices actually preferred in research writing result in a reduction in explicitness. But clausal forms of expression are considerably more explicit than phrasal features, because they grammatically specify the meaning relationships among elements.

Writing, however, is an artificial, conscious activity, and thus it is easy to resist language change in writing... and therefore most written language is an artificial representation, omitting the signs of change which the real language, the spoken one, is full of (McWhorter, 2001, p. 17). The norms of grammatical correctness are in turn assumed to be fixed and resistant to change. And also, the "colloquial" styles over the last century are becoming increasingly prevalent in written discourse (Hundt & Mair, 1999; Leech, Hundt, Mair, & Smith, 2009; Mair, 2006).

As summarized in Table 3.1, linguistic features like attributive adjectives, clausal embedding and noun modification etc. are listed to show in a clearer way of the comparison of the variations of the two types of academic writing.

Table 3.1 **Summary of Major Linguistic Difference Between Text Excerpts**

Humanities	Science
Text Sample 3: literary criticism +attributive adjectives +clausal embedding	Text Sample 4: biochemistry +nominalizations -clausal embedding ++nouns as noun pre-modifiers +appositive noun phrases

Chapter 4
Academic Writing Style, Grammar, and Layout

The style and grammar of academic writing matter very much for accessors; the requirement of having good expression and grammar is present in nearly all marking criteria. Moreover, poor style and grammar will not inhibit clarity.

Take musical performance as an example. If your style is informal or wordy and your writing has many grammatical errors, this is like a performer who has not practiced for a performance. If your writing is incomprehensible, this is like a performer who cannot even play an instrument. Ultimately, you want the accessor or the marker to grasp your meaning without noticing they are reading, just like enjoying a good performance.

This chapter will focus on writing style, grammar advice and the layout of academic writing. A number of errors made by writers will be identified and how they can be fixed will be explained.

4.1 Academic Writing Style

In academic writing, we try to use language which, for the most part, is free from additional meanings or extended meanings and functions. There are some characteristics of academic writing to which we try to conform when writing in an academic context.

4.1.1 Avoid Informality

Informal language should be avoided in academic writing not only because it often performs additional functions, but because, as is the case with slang, the meaning will not be clear to someone who is not a member of a particular group. As is show in Table 4.1, most of the expression problems discussed in the sections have a sense of informality. And the formal equivalents of informal expressions are listed in Table 4.1 as well.

Table 4.1 Some Informal Words and Phrases and Their Formal Equivalents

Informal words or phrases(in italics)	Formal equivalents
The experimenters then *worked out*...	The experimenters then determined...
However, one key aspect of Isabella's case does not *mesh* with her psychologist's diagnosis	However, one key aspect of Isabella's case does not support her psychologist's diagnosis.
This second argument is going to *talk about*...	Second, this essay will consider...
Yong is *basically saying* that…	Yong's point is that...
This idea *comes* from the fact that	This idea derives from the fact that...
The recipients of the medication were *mixed up*.	The recipients of the medication were confused.
This fact should *not be ignored as well*.	This fact should also be considered.
One of the characteristics of a good movie is the extent to which it deals with *front-burner* issues.	One of the characteristics of a good movie is the extent to which it deals with significant issues.

4.1.2 Be Careful When Using Technical Terms or Jargon

Technical terms, or jargons, are words or phrases specific to an area of expertise. The meaning of these words and phrases is usually unclear to common people. Technical terms are useful for experts to communicate. For example, "backend" in computing refers to part of an application that is not seen by the user, and "secondary colors" in art means colors which are created by mixing primary colors. However, technical terms can shift from being a means of making communication between experts more efficient to a kind of formal slang, which are hard for outsiders to understand. Even worse, technical terms that are combined with wordiness will result in weak or unremarkable arguments. As is implied in the "Author Guidelines" for the academic journal *Philosophy and Literature*: "The editors prefer contributions free of jargon or needless technicality. Clarity is one of our ideals." So, in the interest of being able to communicate with as wide an audience as possible, try to minimize the use of technical terms. And if a technical term needs to be used, define it.

4.1.3 Define the Degree of Certainty

Often, the outcome of exploring a complex problem is a statement which cautiously supports or opposes a position. If the reasoning and evidence is strong, match it with language which indicates a high degree of certainty. When reasoning and evidence is weaker, use hedging language to indicate the caution. Hedging language includes words such as "perhaps", "this suggests that", "largely", "it is likely that", "a little", "generally". Example 4.1 demonstrates both good hedging and unhelpful hedging.

Example 4.1 Good Hedging and Unhelpful Hedging

1. Good Hedging

Perhaps the most important role that science fiction can play in human development is inspiring technological advances.

Analysis

While the claim is plausible, many would not agree. Thus, without "Perhaps", a reader who is knowledgeable about science fiction might be more likely to view what follows in a negative way. With "Perhaps", the knowledgeable reader will wait to see what the argument is before making objections.

2. Unhelpful Hedging

Stories of alien invasions seemed to dominate early science fiction movies.

Analysis

"Seemed" is a case of over-hedging. Either stories of alien invasion did or did not dominate early science fiction movies, this could be a fact proved by specific data. Hence the statement doesn't have any point.

4.1.4 Avoid Overly Emotive Language

Sometimes writers are tempted in academic writing to express the feelings about a subject. While doing this is not forbidden, it is not encouraged, unless doing so is part of the assignment (for example, a book review). Remember that academic work is successful when it establishes its points with a base of reasoning and evidence. Showing the care about a subject or preferential attitude to a side of a debate will not gain any credits. None of this is to say that you should not have strong feelings about what you write; rather, you should use your feelings to motivate you to track down good sources and produce compelling arguments. Example 4.2 provides an emotive claim and an improved version of it.

Example 4.2 Too Much Emotion

Emotive version

The unmitigated farce which was the Prime Minister's shabby handling of the tariff negotiations would have been laughable if the political climate had not been so serious.

Analysis

"unmitigated farce", "shabby" and "laughable" all carry too much emotion.

Non–emotive version

The Prime Minister's handling of the tariff negotiations was concerning given the political climate.

Analysis

Here all of the emotive words have been replaced by "concerning". We now expect that further reasoning and evidence will be introduced to support the claim.

4.1.5 Be Wary of Using Poetic Language

Poetic or literary language not only creates the denotational or literal meanings of words, but their connotations. Poetic language is not desirable in academic writing because it can make writing hard to follow or distracting. But this does not mean that the writing needs to be dry. A bit of creatively poetic can be acceptable. But your work must already be academically strong. Example 4.3 contains an instance of unsuccessful poetic language.

To get a sense of successful poetic language in academic writing, see Example 4.4. in which the extract comes from Hurley, Dennett and Adams's book (2011, p. 44).

> Example 4.3 Unsuccessful poetic language
>
> From a student's essay
>
> As one's art is often a reflection of oneself, the ways that extra-terrestrials have been linked onto paper and shown on the silver screen can be explored to reveal the characteristics of the creator.
>
> Analysis
>
> The point that a person's art reflects who they are is certainly worth exploring; however, the poetic phrases "linked onto paper", and "the silver screen" contribute little. Moreover, "the silver screen" is not even poetic.

> Example 4.4 Successful Poetic Language
>
> From an academic book
>
> Release theories construe humor as a form of relief excessive nervous arousal... Release theory has lost popularity for a variety of reasons. In the information age, the metaphor of psychic energy, and the tensions and pressures that build up as this ghostly gasoline accumulates in the imagined plumbing and storage tanks of the mind, seems old-fashioned and naive.
>
> Analysis
>
> The poetic language used here is successful in part because of its gentle mocking of the metaphors used in psychoanalysis.

4.1.6 Avoid Clichés

A cliché is an overused expression. Clichés should be avoided for the following reasons.

- They sound informal because of their overuse, especially in speech.
- Their meaning can be unclear.
- They make the writer seem lazy and unintelligent.

Example 4.5 contains some clichés and improved versions.

Example 4.5 Clichés

Cliché (in italics)	Improved version
First and foremost, this essay will show...	**Most importantly**, this essay will show...
Day after day, things once thought impossible are becoming possible.	We **regularly encounter** things which were once thought impossible becoming possible.
The student needs to *unpack* the term.	The student needs to **explain** what the term means.
These remarks are a *prime* example of...	These remarks are an excellent **example** of...
It is these ideas that researchers need to *bring to the party*.	It is these ideas that researchers need to **include in their work**.

4.1.7 Avoid Wordiness and Repetition

Wordiness means to use too many words to make a point. In academic writing, writers should always try to say what needs to be said with the fewest words possibly.

Repetition can occur when a writer attempts to sound "academic". It also arises in drafting and should be addressed when editing. Example 4.6 contains two instances of wordiness and improved versions.

Example 4.6 Wordiness

Example of wordiness	Improved versions
More than often the notion of X almost always means the use of Y.	Frequently X involves the use of Y.
The idea of the concept should not be understood as referring to...	The concept should not be understood as referring to...

Repetition occurs when two words mean the same thing (for example, "ideas and values") or when the meaning of one word is implied in the meaning of another (for example, "restate again"). If a point needs to be restated in different words, the repetition can be signaled by "in other words" or "that is". Example 4.7 contains some repetitions and improved versions.

Example 4.7 Repetitions

Repetition(in italics)	Improved version
These works *share several things in common.*	These works **share several characteristics.**
Narrow grounds for lifting the corporate veil do exist, but judicial reaction has been seen as *inconsistent and lacks uniformity.*	Narrow grounds for lifting the corporate veil do exist, but judicial reaction has been seen as in**consistent.**
This placed the *responsibility and control* over health and illness within the medical profession.	This placed the **responsibility** for health and illness within the medical profession.
The author writes about people who feel that their lives are *pointless and purposeless.*	The author writes about people who feel that their lives are **purposeless.**

4.1.8 Avoid Using Contractions

A contraction is a type of abbreviation where two words are shortened and combined. Contractions sound spoken and thus informal. There is not a strong case against their use in academic writing, but it is still best to avoid them. So, don't write: it's, don't, can't, isn't, shouldn't, won't, mightn't, could've, doesn't. Instead, write: it is, do not, cannot, is not, should not, will not, might not, could have, and does not.

4.1.9 Be Wary of Using "I"

There is no consensus about whether or not "I" should be used in academic writing. In order not to be subjective and informal, the use of "I" should be avoided. Example 4.8 contains instances where the use of "I" is unnecessary, problematic or successful (Okin, 1999).

Example 4.8 The Use of "I"

1. An Unnecessary Use of "I"

[1] Scholars such as Bruce Sterling take a utilitarian view of the creation of genres, which I support. [2] Sterling rightly asserts that if there is not "a deeper social need" to create a new genre, the genre should not be created.

Analysis

The student makes their opinion clear in the second sentence with the adverb "rightly", and thus the words "which I support" are unnecessary.

2. A Problematic Use of "I"

[1] These accusations merit a thorough assessment of the current legal situation regarding lifting the corporate veil of corporate groups. [2] I will focus on this aspect of the debate in the remainder of this essay.

Analysis

The use of "I" in sentence [2] is problematic, because the sentence could have been phrased differently. For example, "The remainder of this essay will focus on this aspect of the debate."

3. An Academic Use of "I" (Okin, S. M. p.345)

[1] While I cannot here discuss all the relevant dialogues, the following paper attempts, through analysis of Plato's arguments about private property and the family in relation to the polis, to explain why he appears so inconsistent about the nature and the proper role of women. [2] I contend that when one compares the arguments and proposals of the Republic with those of the Laws, it becomes clear that the absence or presence of the private family determines whether Plato advocates putting into practice his increasingly radical beliefs about the potential of women.

Analysis

In sentence [1] Okin could have written, "while this paper cannot" rather than being less engaging. Similarly, sentence [2] could have begun with, "this article contends that", but this wording changes little.

4.2 Grammar

Grammatical errors, particularly common ones that are easily avoided, are often interpreted as a sign that the writer is careless about the essay. Hence, everything in this essay will be viewed with a negative light. Having a marker or viewer of the essay who feels generous when appraising the essay is an asset. Try to use computer programs or apps to check your grammar, and make as few common errors in grammar as possible. Here what is mentioned is one aspect of punctuation and the tense used in academic writing.

4.2.1 Semicolons and Colons

The line between the correct use of semicolons and colons is blurred. We see increasing occasions in which semicolons are used where there should be a colon or comma. Table 4.2 provides some common correct use of semicolon and colon.

Table 4.2 Correct Semicolon and Colon Use

Correct use	Example
Semicolons Can be used to separate two sentences which are closely related in meaning.	The negotiations failed; it seemed there would be no end to the conflict.
Semicolons can be used before a conjunctive adverb. The words include "however", "therefore", and "moreover", but exclude the co-ordinating conjunctions, for example, for, and, nor, but, or, yet, so.	Modi suggested that the policy had been too harsh; however, the consensus was that the policy had been too lenient.
Semicolons should be used in a list containing items which have internal punctuation.	The police examined the man's house; the location where he was last seen was also where his wallet was found; and the garage where he worked.
Use a colon, not a semicolon, to indicate what will follow expands or clarifies what has just been written.	Trang had one desire: to come top of the class.
Similarly, use a colon to introduce a list.	Trang enjoyed the following foods: truffles, capers, olives and artichokes.

4.2.2 Tense

While there are many tenses in English, there are four you will commonly use in your essays: present simple, past simple, present perfect and future simple. Table 4.3 explains and illustrates these tenses.

Table 4.3 Common Tenses in Academic Writing

Tense and description	Example
Use present simple tense when you refer to things that have been written by others, even if they were written long ago.	Plato argues that only once philosophers become rulers will states funtion as they should.
Use past simple tense when you refer to something that actually happened. This could be an outcome of a study or an event.	The researchers found that... In all address to the Queensland obesity summit, Tony Abbott asserted that...
Use present perfect tense when speaking about recent research. This tense implies people have done things in the past and these things continue up to the present. You can also use present perfect tense in your conclusions.	More recently, research has focused on... This essay has argued that...

Use future simple tense when you are outlining what you will go on to discuss.	This essay will argue that...

4.3 Layout

Having a poor layout has a similar effect on a reviewer as making common grammatical errors. Given that there is variability in layout preferences, check requirements before submitting work. Table 4.4 illustrates a number of aspects of layout which is preferred by reviewers.

Table 4.4 Guidelines for Presenting the Essay

Layout aspect	Elaboration
Line space	Use 1.5 or double spacing. Single-spaced assignments are harder to read and write comments on.
Font and font size	Times New Roman is often preferred. Avoid obscure fonts, 11 or 12 point is preferred.
Page numbers	Include page numbers in the essay's footer.
Borders	Do not put borders or other decorations around the essay.
Reference list	Present the reference list on a new page at the end of your essay.

Conclusion

An essay gains a lot of credits from expression, grammar and layout. Once you move beyond essay writing and have to write things such as thesis proposals, journal articles or book chapters, everything relies on your expression, grammar and presentation. Clear, grammatically-correct, well-presented writing creates an excellent impression, whereas even one misused possessive apostrophe can sink the ship. Therefore, more practice will help to get these details right.

Chapter 5
Critique and Synthesis Skills in Academic Writion

When writing papers in college, you are often called on to respond critically or synthetically to source materials. Critical and synthetic reading requires the abilities to summarize and evaluate. A summary is a brief restatement in the reader's own words of the content of the reading material. An evaluation, however, is a more complicated and difficult matter. In an academic work, writers need to read to gain and use new information; but as sources are not equally valid or equally useful, there is a need to distinguish critically among them by evaluating them and summarize synthetically. To become a critical and synthetic reader, one may pose two categories of questions about passages, articles, and books that he/she reads. (1) What is the author's purpose in writing? (2) To what extent do you agree with the author?

5.1 Critical Reading

All critical reading begins with a critical summary. Thus, before attempting an evaluation, the author's purpose, thesis, content and structure must be located. A piece of writing may be informative, persuasive or entertaining. As the focus of this book is on academic writing, this chapter will introduce the criteria for good informative and persuasive writing as these two types of writing are mainly used in academic writing.

5.1.1 Evaluating Informative Writing

A piece intended to inform will provide definitions, describe or report on a process, recount a story, give historical background, and provide facts and figures. An author needs to use verifiable records to provide information. Then, the reader can consider three criteria in response to the writing: accuracy, significance, and fair interpretation of information (Carmel et al., 2007).

Accuracy of Information

One of the responsibilities as a critical reader is to find out if the information presented is accurate. This means one should check facts against other sources. Government publications are often good resources for verifying facts about legislation, population data, official statistics, and the like. Library databases and websites are also good resources for searching key terms. However, since material on the Web is essentially "self-published", one must be very critical in assessing its credibility. A wealth of useful information is now available on the Internet, but there is also a tremendous amount of distorted "facts" and opinions.

Significance of Information

In an informative writing, one may wonder whether the information makes any difference or significance. What can the person who is reading gain from this information? How is knowledge improved by the publication of this material? Is the information of importance to the reader? Why or why not?

Fair Interpretation of Information

Once an author has presented information, he or she will attempt to evaluate or interpret it, since information that has not been evaluated or interpreted is of little use. A critical reader needs to make a distinction between the author's presentation of facts and figures and his or her interpretation of them. Pay attention to whether the logic by which the author connects interpretation with facts is sound. Perhaps the author's conclusions are not justified, and a contrary explanation for the same facts can be drawn.

5.1.2 Evaluating Persuasive Writing

Writing is frequently intended to persuade—that is, to influence the reader's thinking. To make a persuasive writing, the writer must begin with an assertion that is arguable, some statement about which reasonable people could disagree. The assessment of the validity of the argument and the conclusion can be determined by whether the author has clearly defined key terms, used information fairly, argued logically and not fallaciously.

Clearly Defined Terms

The validity of an argument depends to some degree on how carefully an author has defined key terms. If an author writes that "America's elites accepted as a matter of course that a free society can sustain itself only through virtue and temperance in the people"(Murray, 1993), readers need to know what, exactly, the author means by "elites" and by "virtue and temperance" before they can assess the validity of the argument. In such cases, the success of the argument—its ability to persuade—hinges on the definition of a term. So, in responding to an argument, make sure you and the author are clear on what exactly is being argued.

Fair Use of Information

Information is used as evidence in support of arguments. When you encounter such evidence, ask yourself two questions. (1) Is the information accurate and up-to-date? (2) Has the author cited representative information? For instance, it would be dishonest to argue that an economic recession is unavoidable and to cite only indicators of economic downturn while failing to cite contrary and positive evidence.

Logical Argumentation: Avoiding Logical Fallacies

To be convincing, an argument should be governed by principles of logic—clear and orderly thinking. Several examples of faulty thinking and logical fallacies are as follows (Lucas, 2007).

A. Emotionally Loaded Terms

Writers sometimes attempt to sway readers by using emotionally charged words—words with positive connotations to influence readers to their own point of view or words with negative connotations to influence readers away from the opposing point of view. The fact that an author uses emotionally loaded terms does not necessarily invalidate the argument. But when reading academic writing, readers should be sensitive to how emotional terms are being used, particularly sensitive whether they are being used deceptively or to hide the essential facts.

B. Ad Hominem Argument

In an ad hominem argument, the writer rejects opposing views by attacking the person who holds them. By calling opponents' names, an author avoids the issue. Consider the following Example 5.1.

> **Example 5.1**
>
> I could more easily accept my opponent's plan to increase revenues by collecting on delinquent tax bills if he had paid more than a hundred dollars in state taxes in each of the past three years. But the fact isthat he's a millionaire with a millionaire's tax shelters. This man hasn't paid a wooden nickel for the state services he and his family depend on. So I ask you whether he is the one to be talking about taxes to use.

It could well be that the opponent has paid virtually no state taxes for three years; but his fact has nothing to do with, and is wrong to divert attention from, the merits of a specific proposal for increasing revenues. This attack against the man himself violates the principles of logic. Writers must make their points by citing evidence in support of their views and by challenging contrary evidence.

C. False Cause

The fact that one event precedes another in time does not mean that the first event has caused the second. For example, fish begin dying by the thousands in a lake near your hometown. An environmental group immediately cites chemical dumping by several manufacturing plants as the cause.

But other causes are possible: a disease might have affected the fish; the growth of algae might have contributed to the deaths; or acid rain might be a factor. The origins of an event are usually complex and are not always traceable to a single cause. So careful examination of cause-and-effect reasoning is needed. In Latin, this fallacy is known as *post hoc, ergo propter hoc* ("after this, therefore because of this").

D. Either/Or Reasoning

Either/or reasoning also results from an unwillingness to recognize complexity. If an author analyzes a problem and offers only two courses of action, one of which he or she refutes, then you are entitled to object that the other is not thereby true. Usually, several other options are possible. For whatever reason, the author has chosen to overlook them. As an example, suppose you are reading a selection on genetic engineering and the author builds an argument on the basis of the following Example 5.2.

Example 5.2

Research in gene splicing is at a crossroads: Either scientists will be carefully monitored by civil authorities and their efforts limited to acceptable applications, such as disease control; or, lacking regulatory guidelines, scientists will set their own ethical standards and begin programs in embryonic manipulation that, however well intended, exceed the proper limits of human knowledge.

Certainly, other possibilities for genetic engineering exist beyond the two mentioned here. But the author limits debate by establishing an either/or choice. Such limitation is artificial and does not allow for complexity. As a critical reader, be on the alert for either/or reasoning.

E. Hasty Generalization

Writers are guilty of hasty generalization when they draw their conclusions from too little evidence or from unrepresentative evidence. To argue that scientists should not proceed with the human genome project, a recent editorial urged that the project be abandoned is to make a hasty generalization. This editorial may be unrepresentative of the views of most individuals—both scientists and laypeople—who have studied and written about the matter.

F. False Analogy

Comparing one person, event, or issue to another may be illuminating, but it may also be confusing or misleading. Differences between the two may be more significant than the similarities, and conclusions drawn from one may not necessarily apply to the other. A writer who argues that it is reasonable to quarantine people with AIDS because quarantine has been effective in preventing the spread of smallpox is assuming an analogy between AIDS and smallpox that (because of the differences between the two diseases) is not valid.

G. Non Sequitur

Non sequitur is in Latin for "it does not follow"; the term is used to describe a conclusion that does not logically follow from a premise. "Since minorities have made such great strides in the past few decades," a writer may argue, "we no longer need affirmative action programs". Aside from the fact that the premise itself is arguable (have minorities made such great strides?), it does not follow that because minorities may have made great strides, there is no further need for affirmative action programs.

H. Oversimplification

Be alert for writers who offer easy solutions to complicated problems. "America's economy will be strong again if we all 'buy American'", a politician may argue. But the problems of America's economy are complex and cannot be solved by a slogan or a simple change in buying habits. Likewise, a writer who argues that we should ban genetic engineering assumes that simple solutions will be sufficient to deal with the complex moral dilemmas raised by this new technology.

5.2 What Is a Synthesis?

A synthesis is a written discussion that draws on two or more sources. Your ability to write syntheses depends on your ability to infer relationships among sources—essays, articles, fiction, and also non-written sources, such as lectures, interviews, and observations. In fact, if you've written research papers, you've already written syntheses. In an academic synthesis, you make explicit the relationships that you have inferred among separate sources.

Before synthesizing, you must be able to summarize these sources. At the same time, you must go beyond summary to make judgments—judgments based on your critical reading of your sources: what conclusions you have drawn about the quality and validity of these sources, whether you agree or disagree with the point made in your sources and why. Furthermore, you must go beyond the critique of individual sources to determine the relationships among them.

Because a synthesis is based on two or more sources, you will need to be selective when choosing information from each other. As a writer what you must do is to select from each source the ideas and information that best allow you to achieve your purpose.

5.2.1 Purpose

Your purpose in reading source materials and then in drawing on them to write your own material is often reflected in the wording of an assignment. For instance, consider the following assignments on the Civil War in Example 5.3.

> **Example 5.3**
>
> *American History.* Evaluate the author's treatment of the origins of the Civil War.
>
> *Economics.* Argue the following proposition, in light of your readings: "The Civil War was fought not for reasons of moral principle but for reasons of economic necessity."
>
> *Mass Communications.* Discuss how the use of photography during the Civil War may have affected the perceptions of the war by Northerners living in industrial cities.
>
> *Literature.* Select two twentieth-century Southern writers whose work influence you believe is apparent in a novel or a group of short stories written by each author. The works should not be about the civil war.
>
> *Applied Technology.* Compare and contrast the technology of warfare available in the 1860s with the technology available in a century earlier.

Each of these assignments creates for you a particular purpose for writing. Having located sources relevant to your topic, you would select only those parts that helped you in fulfilling this purpose. And how you used those parts, how you related them to other material from other sources, would also depend on your purpose. But because the purposes of these assignments are different, different writers would make different use of the sources. Those same parts or aspects of one source that you find worthy of detailed analysis might be mentioned only in brief by other writers.

5.2.2 Using Your Sources

Your purpose determines not only what parts of your sources you will use but also how you will relate them to one another. Since the very essence of synthesis is the combining of information and ideas, you must have some basis on which to combine them. Some relationships among the materials in your sources must make them worth synthesizing. It follows that the abler you are to discover such relationships, the abler you will be to use your sources in writing syntheses. The mass communication assignment requires you to draw a cause-and-effect relationship amorg photographs of the war. The applied technology assignment requires you to compare and contrast state-of-art weapons technology in the eighteenth and nineteenth centuries. The economics assignment requires you to argue a economic proposition. In each case, your purpose will determine how you relate your source materials to one another. In any event, your purpose determines your essay. Your purpose determines which sources you research, which ones you use, which parts of them you use, at which points in your essay you use them, and in what manner you relate them to one another.

5.2.3. Types of Synthesis: Explanatory and Argument (Behrens, Rosen, & Beedles, 2004)

Synthesis can be categorized into two main types: explanatory and argument. The easiest way to recognize the difference between these two types may be to consider the difference between a newspaper article and an editorial in the same subject. Most likely, we'd say that the main purpose of the newspaper article is to convey information, and the main purpose of the editorial is to convey opinion or interpretation. And this is also essentially the distinction between explanatory and argument syntheses. As a distinction, compare the following two paragraphs as examples.

First Example (Starr & Taggart, 1998)

Example 5.4

Researchers now use recombinant DNA technology to analyze genetic changes. With this technology, they cut and splice DNA from different species, then insert the modified molecules into bacteria or other types of cells that engage in rapid replication and cell division. The cells copy the foreign DNA right along with their own. In short order, huge populations produce quantities of useful recombinant DNA molecules. The new technology also is the basis of genetic engineering, by which genes are isolated, modified, and inserted back into the same organism or into a different one.

Next Example (Rifkin, 1998)

Example 5.5

Many in the life sciences field would have us believe that the new gene-splicing technologies are irrepressible and irreversible and that any attempt to oppose their introduction is both futile and retrogressive. They never stop to even consider the possibility that the new genetic science might be used in a wholly different manner rather than currently being proposed. The fact is that the corporate agenda is only one of two potential paths into the Biotech Century. It is possible that the growing number of anti-eugenic activists around the world might be able to ignite a global debate around alternative uses of the new science—approaches that are less invasive, more sustainable and humane and that conserve and protect the genetic rights of future generations.

Both of these passages deal with the topic of biotechnology, but the two take quite different approaches. The first passage came from a biology textbook, while the second appeared in a magazine article. As we might expect from a textbook on the broad subject of biology, the first passage is explanatory and informative; it defines and explains some of the key concepts of biotechnology without taking a position or providing commentary about the implications of the technology. The magazine article is argumentative or persuasive. Its primary purpose is to convey a point of view regarding the topic of biotechnology.

The primary purpose in a piece of writing is either informative, persuasive, or entertaining or the combination of the three. Some scholars of writing argue that all writing is essentially persuasive, and even without entering into that complex argument, we have just seen how the varying purposes in writing do overlap. In order to persuade others of a particular position we typically must also inform them about it; conversely, a primarily informative piece of writing also must work to persuade the reader that its claims are truthful. Just as distinguishing the primary purpose in a piece of writing helps you to critically read and evaluate it, distinguishing the primary purpose in your own writing helps you to make the appropriate choices regarding your approach.

5.3 Writing of Explanatory Synthesis

An explanation helps readers understand a topic. Writers explain when they divide a subject into its component parts and present them to the reader in a clear and orderly way. Explanations may entail descriptions that recreate in words some object, place, emotion, event, sequence of events, or state of affairs. Your job in writing an explanatory paper is not to argue a particular point, but rather to present the facts in a reasonably objective manner. Of course, explanatory papers should be based on a thesis. But the purpose of a thesis in an explanatory paper is to release a particular opinion rather than to focus the various facts contained in the paper (Carmel et al., 2007).

Guidelines for Writing Synthesis

- Consider your purpose in writing.
- Select and carefully read your sources. Identify those aspects or parts of the sources that will help you fulfill your purpose.
- Take notes on your reading. This will help you in formulating your thesis statement, and in choosing and organizing your sources later.
- Formulate a thesis. Your thesis is the main idea that you want to present in your synthesis. Predrafting about the ideas discussed in the readings is needed to work out the thesis.
- Decide how you will use your source material.
- Develop the organization.
- Write the first draft. As you write, you may discover new ideas and make room for them by adjusting the outline.
- Document your sources. Don't open yourself to charges of plagiarism.
- Revise your synthesis. Make sure that the synthesis reads smoothly, logically, and clearly from beginning to end. Check for grammatical correctness, punctuation, and spelling.

5.4 Writing of Argument Synthesis

In contrast to an explanatory thesis, an argumentative thesis is persuasive in purpose. Writers working with the same source material might conceive of and support opposing theses. So, the thesis for an argument synthesis is a claim about which reasonable people could disagree. It is a claim with which—given the right arguments—your audience might be persuaded to agree. The strategy of your argument synthesis is therefore to find and use convincing support for your claim. One way of looking at an argument is to see it as a combination of three essential elements: claim, support, and assumption. A claim is a proposition or conclusion that you are trying to prove. You prove this claim by using support in the form of fact or expert opinion. Linking your supporting evidence to your claim is your assumption about the subject. By nature, assumptions tend to be more general than either claims or supporting evidence.

Here are the examples of essential elements of an argument.

Claim

High school students should be restricted to no more than two hours of TV viewing every day.

Support

An important new study and the testimony of educational specialists reveal that students who watch more than two hours of TV a night have, on average, lower grades than those who watch less TV.

Assumption

Excessive TV viewing negatively affects academic performance.

As another example, the following is a claim suitable for an argument synthesis.

Claim

Computer mediated communication threatens to undermine human intimacy, connection, and ultimate community.

The following are the supports that can be used to support the claim.

Support

(1) While the Internet presents us with increased opportunities to meet people, these meetings are limited by geographical distance.

(2) People are spending increasing amounts of time in cyberspace. In 1998, the average Internet user spent over four hours per week online, a figure that has nearly doubled recently.

(3) College health officials report that excessive Internet usage threatens many college students' academic and psychological well-being.

(4) Communication skills used and the connections formed during Internet contact fundamentally differ from those used and formed during face-to-face contact.

And the assumptions should be constructed logically and rationally by linking the supporting facts or experts' opinions.

Chapter 6
Visual Skills in Academic Writing

Scientific reports rely heavily on presenting information visually. Tables, charts, graphs, sketches, photographs, and illustrations or line drawings are the staples of scientific communication. Scientists expect visual representations of information.

Photographs or illustrations obviously are meant to represent faithfully what is visible. They bear witness to what the researchers themselves have observed. But this is also true for the other sorts of visual elements that accompany a good report: charts, graphs, figures, tables, and line drawings all have the purpose of bearing witness to an empirical observation, sometimes enhanced to clarify the important relations.

The most common purpose of an illustration is to represent numerical data from measurements taken in an experiment. Those numerical data often have to be subjected to various kinds of statistical manipulations before they make sense of anything from simple averaging, to being crunched through complex mathematical formulas by a computer.

There are two primary reasons for choosing to present information visually.

(1) One is to make the analysis of information easier and to describe relationships among data that are not clear enough through other means.

(2) The other iis to communicate visual aspects of a phenomenon or a device.

When using visual testimony, keep in mind that, though, communicating information this way may simplify the message, arranging data into charts or graphs and producing line drawings can be time-consuming and expensive. If you are considering publishing your work, you should know that editors do not like unnecessary figures and illustrations because of the expense they add to publication. Moreover, a poor illustration will only confuse and frustrate the reader. However, if you believe that the purpose of your illustration is to offer necessary witness, then you can choose wisely among formats for presenting data (Carmel et al., 2007).

> Principles for All Visuals
> - Use visuals when they simplify information; that is, on occasions when words alone convey the information less efficiently and concisely.
> - Information presented in a visual form should supplement, not duplicate, information presented in the writing.
> - All visuals should be self-contained. They should reveal important information without reference to the body of the writing.
> - All visuals should be followed by a caption which directs the reader's attention to important aspects of the data or picture and explains them.
> - All visuals should include numbers, and clear labels.
> - Every illustration should be cited in the text.

For instance, by a pie chart (see Figure 6.1), readers instantly know that they will be looking at the divisions of a whole. By contrast, a bar chart emphasizes comparisons of actual values (see Figure 6.2).

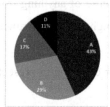
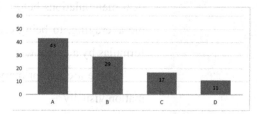

Figure6.1   The pivisions of awhole   **Figure6.2   Comparisons of Actual Values**

6.1 Purpose of Using Visual Presentations

Visual arrangement of information should make information easier to understand. This can be illustrated with something as simple as a basic table. Imagine that a meteorologist measures temperature in a controlled environment simulator at varying time intervals beginning at time $t_0=0:00$. There are many ways the author could present relevant information, but here are three examples.

A. t_0(time)= 0: 00, T (temperature °c) = 9 °C

t_1=10:05, T_1=18 ℃; t_2=12:08, T_2=25 ℃; t_3=18:23, T_3=16 ℃; t_4=23:32, T_4=11 ℃.

Time	Temperature
0: 00	9 ℃
10: 05	18 ℃
12: 08	25 ℃
18: 23	16 ℃
23: 32	11 ℃

B.

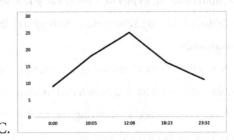

C.

Which of these, A~C, is easiest to understand? Of the three, A makes the reader work hardest just to sort out the data and their relationships. It was easiest for the author to create, however, and would be cheapest for a journal to publish. B simplifies the data enormously, just by the simple trick of arranging the data in columns and rows. It was easy to produce on a word processing program and would not be hard to reproduce in a journal. Yet, it requires of the reader to make at least one step of analysis: scanning the row of figures and abstracting from them the downward trend. Clearly, C has immediate visual impact. It shows forcibly both the trend in the data and the nature of the trend without any further analysis by the reader: the temperature changes according to different time of a day. It also lets the author demonstrate a further level of analysis of the data: the average rate line does not intersect all the data points but rather, abstracts a trend from that data.

The author of the article has to consider a few questions before going through the extra labor of transforming the simple presentation of data in a table B to the more elaborate presentation of the data in the Graph C.

- **How much easier will you make it on the reader by plotting a graph?**

Graph C reveals the crucial trend in data at a single glance, while simple conclusion can be derived quickly from Table B. Whether it is necessary to make a graph when a table can make the point clearly is the question the author need to consider.

- **Are there other relationships you wish to present on the same graph that would require other tables or charts?**

If so, then it might be worth graphing the data points. If not, then a table will probably enough.

- **Are exact values important?**

If so, Table B is more suitable than Graph C, which requires that the reader track values on the exact number instead of just the value represented by a curve line.

The characteristics and the usage of different visual tools will be presented in the following comparison (Clark & Pointon, p. 342).

> **Comparisons of Types of Visual Presentations**
> - Tables or lists are simple ways to organize the precise data points themselves in one-on-one relationships.
> - A graph is best at showing the trend or relationship between two dimensions, or the distribution of data points in a certain dimension.
> - A pie chart is best at showing the relative areas, volumes, or amounts into which a whole (100%) has been divided.
> - Flow charts show the organization or relationships of discrete parts of a system.
> - Photographs are not very good at calling attention. They are best at presenting overall shapes, shades, and relative positionings, or when a "real-life" picture is necessary.
> - Illustrations suit most purposes for representing real objects or the relationship of parts in a large object.

6.2 General Guidelines for Using Visual Presentations

TABLES

Tables are rows and columns of data showing their relationships. If you want to design a table, the following guidelines are for your reference(Clark & Pointon).

> **Guidelines for Composing Tables**
> - Each table is as "Table XX: Title".
> - Be sure to cite every table in the text.
> - Give each table a caption.
> - Use clear and concise column headings.
> - Type a thick or double horizontal line below the headings and at the end of the table.
> - Align data in the field according to decimal places. Do not center numbers if that will offset them from decimal alignment.
> - If data in the field have been assessed statistically, give means, scientific deviations, or errors in footnotes.
> - Double-check data with your presentation of them in the text.

GRAPHS

A bar graph shows the relative proportions of data. Each bar represents one or more divisions of data.

Scatter graphs are plots of individual data points, represented by dots, each of which shows a relationship between two variables. This is effective in showing the distribution of data for which no simple mathematical relationship is immediately apparent by looking at the raw number (see Figure 6.3).

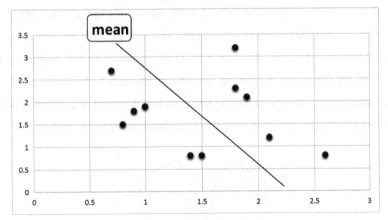

Figure6.3   Seatter Graphs

Line graphs show individual points, each of which represents a relationship between two variables, and then shows the lines between them in order to demonstrate a trend. Line graphs can also plot a continuous relationship between two variables in continuous tracings of data on a graph (see Figure 6.4).

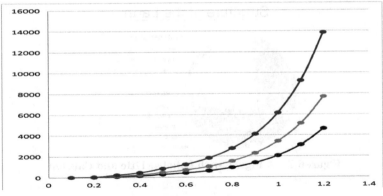

Figure6.4   Line Graphs

CHARTS/COMPUTER FLOWCHARTS

Charts or schematic diagrams are usually boxes around the text or symbols with lines between them, sometimes with arrows, showing relationships. Because they represent abstractions, charts provide a great service to the reader by making those relationships concrete (see Figure 6.5).

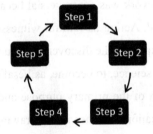

Figure 6.5   Charts/Compurter Flowcharts

ILLUSTRATIONS, DIAGRAMS, AND LINE DRAWINGS

Illustrations and line drawings depict the important aspects of a real phenomenon or system. You should think of them as something between a blueprint and a cartoon. They are not meant to show every part of an object, but only its noticeable features. They generally do not exaggerate proportions.

Line drawings are very good at showing anatomical relations and models, particularly models of intangible or microscopic objects. Scientific texts use line drawings and schematic diagrams most frequently to show machinery, apparatus, or parts of a real object (see Figure 6.6).

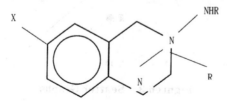

Figure6.6 Line Drawings

Figure 6.7 based on the source from Wikipedia, uses clear labels, and includes a figure title and an explicit caption, even if the caption is redundant of material stated in the body of the article (Wikipedia).

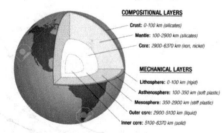

Figure6.7 A Figure with Labebs, Title and Caption

6.3 Conclusion

In his article "Faithful Witness", Alan Burdick, an editor of *The Sciences*, relates this anecdote about one of the origins of scientific illusions (Burdick, 1990).

Andreas Vesalius "*De humani corporis fabrica*" was the first anatomy textbook ever accompanied by detailed illustrations. His work was controversial because it exploded many myths about how the human body was structured. Acting as faithful witnesses, the Vesalian illustrations made even the most distant reader a participant in the discovery. Through them, the claims of a solo anatomist extended to the public realm of science, to become, as Vesalius said, "common property."

This is an excellent description of the primary purpose and function of any good visual representation in a scientific communication, whether it is a drawing, a photograph, or an illustration. All illustrations present testimony about an empirical observation or a set of observations.

Chapter 7
Content in academic writing

The advice about the type of content that is relevant to each chapter of academic writing depends on the purposes or functions of each chapter. Authors must have their understanding of the purposes or functions of the chapter they are about to write, and have their understanding of the types of content that will meet the purposes/functions that have been discussed. It is more often the case that authors have only a partial understanding of the content areas that are typically expected. This chapter begins with explanations of the genre of each part of academic writing. Then, the second part of this chapter outlines the advice on the purposes/functions of each part of a dissertation, and on the content units which meet the purposes/functions that have been discussed. The purpose/function and the content units of these aspects for each of the key chapters of an academic article include introduction, literature review one or more chapters, methodology one or more chapters, presentation of results, discussion of results, conclusion. The third part of this chapter refers to several strategies that can be used in the writing of each chapter of the dissertation. At last, the feedbacks that supervisors usually will give to student authors will be provided.

7.1 Role of Genre Knowledge

The term "genre" has been defined in a number of ways but, in each full definition, a number of key characteristics have always been included. The first is that a genre is a type of discourse that typically occurs in a particular setting. In this case, the particular setting is an academic setting which is defined by the academic community of researchers, teachers, examiners, supervisors and institutions. The second characteristic is the distinctive and recognizable patterns and norms in academic discourse. This means that the type of content presented in one dissertation will be sufficiently similar to that found in other dissertations even when disciplinary and institutional differences are obvious. The third characteristic is the specific purposes and functions that determine the nature of the content and how it is organized.

In order to meet the specific purposes/functions, series of discourse content units that can be included to meet academic genres in each part of a dissertation are proposed here (Bitchener, 2018). When giving students advice about these content units, supervisors need to explain that they are optional (rather than mandatory requirements) about what has typically been observed in research. From the discipline-specific content research that has been published, more generic characteristics have been proposed in a number of books (Bitchener, 2010; Paltridge & Starfield, 2007) and it is these that are outlined in this chapter. These, then, are a starting point for students as they think about the type of content that they may wish to include in their dissertation chapters. Supervisors would do well to discuss academic writing expectations and requirements with all students as part of the advice they give before writing begins.

7.2 Discourse Content Unit Options for Each Dissertation Chapter

7.2.1 The Introduction Chapter

The discourse content unit options of a typical dissertation introduction chapter are presented respectively in Box 7.1 and Table 7.1. It is important to notice that the purposes or functions of an introductory chapter are discussed before the content unit options because they inform the type of content that is appropriate for achieving these purposes and functions

---

Box7.1 Purposes/Functions of an Introduction Chapter

1. Describe the dissertation problem, issue or question that interests you.
2. Review the background and context of the problem.
3. Establish what has been said and done in the problem area by referring to the theoretical, empirical and non-research literature.
4. Identify gaps in the body of knowledge.
5. Explain what you hope to add to this body of knowledge.
6. Explain why the gaps selected for investigation are important/ significant enough for investigation.
7. Outline how you carried out your investigation, together with an indication of the scope and parameters of the research.
8. Outline the content and structure of the dissertation.

In discussing the eight purposes or functions, it is worth highlighting a few points that should be made aware of. First, gaps in the body of knowledge should not only focus on gaps in empirical knowledge but also on theoretical and methodological gaps that may not have been considered or published in earlier literature. Second, because adding to the body of knowledge requires that an original contribution be made, consideration should therefore be given to ways in which the research may be able to contribute to theory-building and to an understanding of effective methodological approaches for investigating the type of problem at the center of the research. Third, in discussing the scope and parameters of the research, students should be acquainted with the fact that their study is a finite piece of investigation and that its parameters need to be clearly identified and justified.

The discourse content unit options in Table 7.1 may guide students in their selection of content for the chapter. The sub-units indicate how the three main units may be discussed. To some extent, they are sequenced to suggest how the argument might be organized.

Table 7.1 The Discourse Content Unit Options of an Introduction Chapter

Main units	Sub–units
1. Establish a research territory	a. Explain the extent to which it is important, central, interesting, problematic or relevant.
	b. Provide background information about the area.
	c. Introduce and review aspects of previous literature in the area(theoretical, empirical and non-research literature).
	d. Define terms and constructs on first mention.

Main units	Sub–units
2. Establish a research gap in the territory	a. Indicate a gap in the literature.
	b. Raise a question about a gap in the literature.
	c. Identify a problem or need.
	d. Extend previous knowledge.
3. Occupy the research gap	a. Outline the purpose, aim, objectives of the research study.
	b. Specify the research questions, hypotheses that were investigated.
	e. Outline the relevant theoretical framewouks and perspectives, positions.
	d. Describe the methodology, design of the study.
	e. Indicate the scope and parameters of the study.
	f. Explain the likely contribution and value of the research to the field of knowledge.
	g. Outline the chapter organization of the study.

There are a number of additional pieces of advice when we explain the discourse content unit options in Table 7.1. First, terms and constructs, as they are used in the dissertation, need to be clearly defined in the introduction. Sometimes students will provide a quotation from an expert in the field to indicate the defining features of the term or construct, but it may not necessarily capture exactly how it has been used in the dissertation research. It may be better for students to write their own definitions and direct the reader forward to the literature review chapter if a wider discussion of the terms and constructs are discussed there. The second additional piece of advice concerns the need to critically assess or evaluate every piece of descriptive literature that is presented, especially when there is some debate about different theoretical positions in the published literature. The third piece of advice relates to main Unit 3. Some disciplines may not expect that all the sub-units be covered in the introductory chapter, so it is important to know what is expected.

7.2.2 The Literature Review Chapter

In discussing the purposes/functions of a dissertation literature review, presented in Box 7.2, it is important to know in which these are similar and different to those outlined for the introductory chapter. Some clarification about the first three purposes or functions may be required. Purpose 1 refers to the empirical literature while purpose 2 refers to the theoretical literature and purpose 3 refers to any other type of literature that may be relevant to the background knowledge that the student believes the readers will need to be informed about (historical documents, reports from organizations, socio-political texts or policies, etc.). Second, informing readers about competing ideas, theories, and findings are an important part of establishing why the student's research is considered important and likely to make a contribution to the field. This is especially important with respect to resolving controversies. The final point to emphasize when discussing the purposes and functions of the literature review is the need for purpose 7 to be explicit about the connection between research questions/hypotheses and the literature that has been presented.

Box7.2 Purposes/Functions of a Literature Review Chapter

1. Review the research literature relevant to the study.
2. Review the theoretical perspectives that underpin or inform the research.
3. Review any non-research literature (reports, etc.) that summarizes and synthesizes background and contextual information.
4. Critique 1~3 above by identifying arguments for/against issues and controversies, and by weighing up the value of various theories, arguments, claims, conclusions, methodologies/designs (including an identification of strengths and weaknesses).
5. Identify gaps or shortcomings in this knowledge.
6. Justify why the gap(s) are important and significant enough.

In discussing the discourse content unit options of the literature review (identified in Table 7.2), supervisors should draw their students' attention to similarities with the discourse content unit options of the introductory chapter.

The content unit options (Box 7.2) provide a macro view of what the content of the literature will include but they do not tell the student much about the specific areas of content that might be included. Students need to come up with a detailed table of contents about what they plan to include and then have a discussion with supervisors about what has been suggested, about the organization of the various suggestions, and about any additional sections or sub-sections they should consider including. Perhaps the most important discussion to have is about how the areas of selected content are going to be organized to create an argument that leads to a position that informed the need for some aspect of the research.

Because knowledge critique is so important and is typically so poorly done, advice should be given to students before they write their literature review about what it means to critique the ideas and findings of others and about why it is important.

The relative importance of the three main discourse moves of literature reviews in the discipline should also be discussed because often the third content unit may only occupy one or two paragraphs at the end of the literature review rather than a lengthier statement. Supervisors should clarify what the expectations of their discipline are.

Table 7.2 The Discourse Content Unit Options of a Literature Review Chapter

Main units	Sub–units
1. Establish some aspect of the knowledge territory relevant to your research.	a. Present knowledge claims and statements about theories, beliefs, constructs and definitions.
	b. Explain the centrality, importance or significance of the area of knowledge.
	c. Present the research evidence (e. g. findings, methodology).
2. Create a research gap in knowledge.	a. Critique knowledge claims, issues, problems associated with Unit 1 claims, present research evidence to support each critique.
	b. Identify gaps in knowledge / research.
	c. Explain any development of traditions that have been established but not fully investigated.
	d. Present arguments for introducing any new perspective or theoretical framework(as a result of Unit 1 claims).
3. Announce how you will occupy the research gap.	a. Announce the aim(s) of your study.
	b. Announce the relevant framework(s).
	c. Announce the key research design and processes.

It is useful to note that the first two main units will comprise a number of relevant and related sections, with each focusing on a major area of literature that is relevant to the background of the research questions/hypotheses.

7.2.3 The Methodology Chapter

Students are likely to be familiar with the content of methodology chapters either from their reading of other dissertations or from their reading of journal articles that report empirical research. The following purposes or functions in Box 7.3 are unlikely to be misunderstood.

Box7.3 Purposes/Functions of a Methodology Chapter

1. Describe and justify the methodological approach best suited to your research questions/hypotheses.

2. Describe and justify the research design best suited to examine your research questions/hypotheses.

3. Describe and justify the specific methods employed for data collection.

4. Explain how the validity and reliability or truthfulness of your data were achieved.

> 5. Describe and justify your data collection procedures.
> 6. Describe and justify your data analysis procedures.

It is useful to discuss some of the discourse content unit options included in Table 7.3 because students and supervisors may have different understandings of what is intended. First, the methodological approach component of the chapter should include a discussion of why it is the appropriate approach for the types of research questions/hypotheses that were investigated. This may lead to a discussion about why a mixed methods approach, a qualitative approach or a quantitative approach was employed and then to an outline of the specific methods that were used to obtain data for answering the research questions or for testing any hypotheses.

Table 7.3 The Discourse Content Unit Options of a Methodology Chapter

Main units	Sub-units
1. Present the procedures for measuring the variables of your research.	a. Describe and justify the methodological approach of the study from a philosophical perspective.
	b. Define, describe and justify the methods of measuring the variables of your study.
2. Explain the data collection procedures.	a. Describe the sample(e. g. location, size, characteristics, context, ethical issues).
	b. Describe the instruments used for data collection, describe the validity and reliability or truthfulness measures.
	c. Describe the steps of the data collection procedures.
	d. Justify a~c, highlighting advantages and disadvantages, in light of research aim (s) and research questions, hypotheses.
3. Explain the data analysis procedures.	a. Describe, illustrate and justify the data analysis procedures.

Furthermore, because this is an academic writing, students are expected to demonstrate the depth of their knowledge. Thus, for example, if they are describing and justifying the statistics they used to determine the significance of their findings, they will be expected to not only describe the tests that were used but also to justify why they were the appropriate ones for the data of the study.

Readers of a methodology chapter should feel confident that they would be able to replicate the study if they chose to. This means that all steps need to be identified. It is important to mention this because a critical piece of information often is left out that is needed so that step 2 can follow on from step 1.

7.2.4 The Presentation of Results Chapter

There is nothing difficult to understand about the purposes/functions of a chapter such as presented in Box7.4 that simply presents the findings or results of the research.

> **Box7.4 Purposes/Functions of a Results Chapter**
>
> 1. Present the results/findings of your study that are relevant to the research questions/hypotheses.

2. Explain what the findings mean (without interpretation and discussion).

3. Present evidence in support of the findings.

A chapter that simply presents results or findings is not difficult to write if a decision has been made about how various findings are to be reached. A discussion about whether they will be presented chronologically according to the order of the research question/hypothesis or in a thematic way would be worth having before students start to write the chapter. Students should be advised to avoid discussing the findings if the chapter is solely about presenting what the findings were.

Main Unit 1, in Table 7.4, suggests that meta-textual information might be provided at the beginning of the chapter. This would be given because readers who read the results chapter before reading any other chapters are reminded of background information. Some supervisors may advise against using this background information because readers to refer back to it in an earlier chapter.

Table 7.4 The Discourse Content Unit Options of a Results Chapter

Main units	Sub–units
1. Present briefly any meta-textual information.	a. Present any back ground information, methodological detail, references forward to the discussion chapter and links between sections that contextualize the results to be presented.
	b. Define, describe and justify the methods of measuring the variables of your study.
2. Present the results..	a. Restate the research question/hypothesis.
	b. Present briefly any important procedures for generating the results that the reader should be reminded of.
	c. Present each result.
	d. Provide evidence for each result (e. g. statistics, examples, tables, figures).
	e. Explain what each result means.

7.2.5 The Discussion of Results Chapter

The first purpose stated in Box7.5 leads the other two main purposes (2 and 3). Having presented the findings of the investigation in the previous chapter, the discussion chapter can then focus on why the findings occurred as they did and on how they might compare with those of other related studies introduced in the literature review chapter. Students should be clear that such a discussion will not only refer to empirical studies but also consider theoretical and methodological explanations associated with studies.

Box7.5 Purposes/Functions of a Discussion of Results Chapter

1. Provide a brief overview of the aim(s) of the research, of the theoretical and research contexts of the research and of the methodological approach for investigating the research questions/hypotheses.

2. Interpret your results, compare them with other research results, and explain why they occurred as they did.

> 3. Discuss the contribution you believe your results have made to the research questions/hypotheses, to theory-building, to new empirical knowledge and to practice.

The range of discourse content unit options outlined in Table 7.5 provides specific guidance on what is typically included in a discussion of findings chapter. Again, the first unit provides a contextual introduction that may or may not be considered necessary. Depending on the importance and significance of a finding, in relation to the focus of the research question, some of the sub-unit options may not be relevant. For example, sub-unit (g) on making suggestions for further research and sub-unit (h) on justifying why further research is recommended may be more relevant to a discussion of several findings than to a discussion of an individual finding. So, it is necessary to consider each of the sub-unit options and reach a decision about why each one should or should not be included in the discussion. Finally, in fact, these sub-units have been sequenced in a logic way.

Table 7.5 The Discourse Content Unit Options of a Discussion of Results Chapter

Main units	Sub-units
1. Provide any background infonilation considered important for understanding the discussion.	a. Restate aim (s), research questions, hypotheses, key research and methodological approach.
2. Present a statement of result.	a. Restate a key result.
	b. Expand statement about the key result.
3. Evaluate / comtrlent on each result.	a. Explain the result by suggesting reasons for it.
	b. Explain whether the result was expected or unexpected.
	c. Compare the result with the results of previous research.
	d. Provide examples of the result.
	e. Make a more general claim arising from the result, draw a conclusion or state a hypothesis.
	f. Quote previous research to support(e).
	g. Make suggestions for further research.
	h. Justify which further research is recommended.

7.2.6 The Conclusion Chapter

It is often the case that the conclusion chapter is read in isolation from other chapters by both students and academics. The reason is that readers want an overview of the dissertation in order to decide whether or not they will read the whole work. Conclusion may be an overview of what has been provided in the discussion chapter. This part of the academic writing is often the most important part because it tells the reader what the research has to offer the field of knowledge. Given its importance, it is surprising that many fail to give it the recognition and attention it needs. See the purposes/functions of a conclusion chapter in Box 7.6 and the discourse content unit options of a conclusion chapter in Table 7.6.

> **Box7.6 Purposes/Functions of a Conclusion Chapter**
> 1. Remind the reader of the aim(s), research questions/hypotheses and methodological

features of your study.

2. Summarize your key findings.

3. Evaluate the importance and significance of your study with a commentary on its contribution to the field (i.e. theory-building, new empirical knowledge, methodological advancements, and practice).

4. Identify limitations of the study (both in terms of weaknesses/flaws and scope/parameters).

5. Identify areas for further research.

6. Identify practical applications.

Table 7.6 The Discourse Content Unit Options of a Conclusion Chapter

Main units	Sub–units
1. Restate aims and a methodological approach of the study.	a. Restate the aim(s), research questions, hypotheses.
	b. Restate key features of the research methodology and methods.
2. Summarize key results.	a. Provide a summary of the key findings of the study.
3. Evaluate the study's contribution to the field (theory, new knowledge, methodology and practice).	a. Comment on the significance of the study for theory-building, developing new empirical knowledge, developing new methodological approaches and for practical application.
	b. Justify each comment.
4. Identify limitations and areas for further research.	a. Identify any limitations (weaknesses/flaws and scope/parameters).
	b. Recommend and justify areas for further research.

7.2.7 The Abstract

The purposes and discourse content unit options of the abstract have been placed at the end of this session because the abstract lies outside the dissertation itself and because it is typically written towards the end of the writing journey. The five purposes identified in Box 7.7 are intended to give a clear overview of the focus of the dissertation. Some disciplines highlight the importance of some of these purposes more than others. In some disciplines, for example, purposes 2 and 5 may be omitted altogether. Purposes 3 and 4 are typically considered of much importance.

Box 7.7 Purposes/Functions of an Abstract

1. Outline the aims of the study.

2. Describe the background and context of the study.

3. Describe the methodology and methods used in the study.

4. Present the key findings of the study.

5. Comment on the contribution of the study to the field of.

If the range of discourse sub-unit options listed in Table 7.7 were to be included in an abstract, it is likely that the text would cover two or three pages. Thus, advice may need to be given about which of these are considered to be more important in the discipline. Typically, main Unit 2, 3, 4 are the most essential content in an abstract. And also, some of the sub-unit options can, of course, be combined within a single statement. The writing of an abstract requires a level of skill that writers may struggle with, so, even though the abstract text is much smaller than that of the other texts they will have written, supervisors and students should be concerned with its difficulties.

Table 7.7 The Discourse Content Unit Options of an Abstract

Main units	Sub-units
1. Introduction	a. Outline background, context of the study.
	b. Explain the motivation for the research.
	c. Explain the significance and centrality of the research focus.
	d. Identify the knowledge gap (s) or need for the continuation of a tradition.
2. Purpose	a. Identify the aims or intentions or research questions/hypotheses.
	b. Develop aspects of (a).
3. Method	a. Identify and justify the methodological approach and methods.
	b. Identify key design aspects.
	c. Identify data sources.
	d. Identify data analysis processes.
4. Product	a. Present main findings of research questions/hypotheses.
5. Conclusion	a. Suggest significance/importance of the findings to the field.
	b. Identify any important limitations.
	c. Make recommendations for further research.

7.3 Strategies for Writing of Each Chapter

The focus of this chapter has been on the purposes/functions of each chapter and on the type of content that each of the chapters may include. Guidelines on the type of content or the areas of content that might be expected in each chapter have also been provided in the form of discourse content unit options. For some people, this advice may be a little too abstract or theoretical so that the rest of this chapter offers some concrete advice.

7.3.1 Analyze Model Examples

Model examples of sections of a chapter, or of a whole chapter, can either be given to students or they can be asked to select one or more from their reading program. The effective approach is to bring the models together for a session in which sections or chapter samples are analyzed and discussed. This means that students need to have reflection upon what they consider to be noteworthy features of the content. It is important that the discussion of the sample text includes reference to the discourse content unit options. An example of this can be found in Bitchener (2010) where parts of chapters are discussed in terms of the extent to which they illustrate the use of a particular discourse units and its various sub-units. For some students, it may be helpful to study a small piece of text and discuss a discourse unit analysis that has been undertaken of that piece of text before giving students the opportunity to do the same with another small piece of text. This can be done in pairs or in small groups. This approach should ensure that students clearly understand what is involved in the approach.

7.3.2 Create a Table of Contents

The creation and discussion of a table of contents is essential to ensure that students are going to focus on content that is relevant to the purposes/functions of the chapter that they are planning to write. The more detailed the table is, the more headings and sub-headings there are. If there is any doubt about this, it may be useful if the student writes up one part of the table of contents first and then seeks the supervisor's feedback before writing the other parts listed in the table of contents.

7.4 Suggestions on Selection of Content for Each Dissertation Chapter

This chapter focuses on the suggestions needed about the selection of content that they have included in their chapters. The amount of feedback that may need to be provided on a chapter will often depend on when the chapter has been written. Early drafts are likely to require more feedbacks and it is for this reason that it is probably best to focus only on the selection of content first rather than focusing on other areas of concern. As each new version is completed, less and less suggestions should be required on the selection of content. The suggestion that is often given on the early drafts of the six chapters of an academic article is discussed in this chapter.

7.4.1 The Introduction Chapter

Students will often write an initial draft of their introduction chapter after they have completed the literature review and before the research data have been collected and analyzed. The reason for this is to ensure that the literature students read does not lead to any necessities of re-collecting new data. The second version of introduction will be written after the results chapter has been written and before the findings are discussed. This is to ensure that the results are added to the revision version of introduction so that it can then be referred to in the discussion of the findings. This is to ensure that each of these chapters aligns with the focus of the other. So, what are the content selection issues that are necessary to be provided with suggestions?

The nature and scope of the problem that the research investigates

Defining and explaining clearly the problem that the research investigates can be a challenge for academic writers. This may be because they are unclear themselves and need to do more reading. However, this issue can be resolved once it has been pointed out as an issue by the supervisor, or when more reading has been completed. Asking questions about what is meant by the terms and/or constructs that they have referred to can also help this process. Discussion of how the scope of the problem could be narrowed to something that is more manageable is helpful too. Discussing the research questions that they plan to investigate helps students to sharpen their understanding of the focus of the problem that informs the various research questions. This discussion can also lead to an elimination of some of the questions and some of the components of irrelevant questions.

The importance or significance of the problem

Being able to articulate the reason(s) for focusing on a particular problem is important if the purpose of the writing is to investigate not only a gap in knowledge but also to advance new knowledge in the field. Sometimes not every gap or issue is worth investigating. In the first instance, if students have not thought carefully about the importance or significance of the problem they have identified and have not explained this clearly and completely enough in their introduction, this is a defect in their introduction. Most often, at this stage of their thinking, students are able to make one or two reasonable points about ways in which they think their research may be significant for the field. A further discussion of these points can lead to a realization that there are other ways in which their findings may also be significant.

How the problem is investigated

Once the problem has been identified, described and justified as one that is worthy of investigation, the introduction chapter should signal the key aims or the research questions/hypotheses of the study. The overview of how the problem is to be carried out tends to vary from discipline to discipline, with some requiring a relatively detailed introduction to the key components of the methodology chapter and others requiring only a sentence or two that directs readers to what is presented at the end of the literature review chapter(s) or in the methodology chapter itself.

The contribution to the field

Perhaps, this is the most important part of the introduction chapter but, unfortunately, it tends to be the most frequently ignored or the most poorly considered. While it is understood that students will increase their understanding of the significance of their work, it should still be possible for them to state some goals in terms of what they believe their original contribution might be or in terms of new empirical knowledge and methodological contributions, even if the understanding of their contribution to theory-building is tentative. At least, an early draft of the introduction chapter should be able to identify what the student hopes to add to the body of knowledge. Students need to think about the contribution to the field before starting writing.

7.4.2 The Literature Review Chapter

The literature review may be presented in one or more chapters. In Social Sciences and Humanities, it often occupies two chapters, with one being devoted to the theoretical conceptualization of the research and the other to the empirical and non-research components of the research. Depending on how thorough their reading has been and how effective their review of the reading has been, these two factors will determine the nature and amount of feedback they are given on the first full writing of the literature review.

The literature review is typically regarded as the most difficult chapter for students to write, not only because it serves a variety of purposes and covers a large amount of text but also because it draws upon a wide range of reading, thinking and writing skills, not to mention a critical viewpoint with regard to the literature that is presented. It is necessary to give feedback on the first full draft, which is discussed now in this section. As we saw in the previous section on the introduction chapter, macro issues are best dealt with first.

The selection of content

First and foremost, the content needs to be relevant to the focus of the problem or the research questions. therefore, the content may include non-research literature (e.g. reports, documents related to the wider context of the subject of the research) as well as research literature (both theoretical and empirical). The consideration of the theoretical perspectives relevant to the focus of the research is often more of a challenge for some students. Suggestions on the latter may often include not only guidance on what theoretical literature to consider from within the field in which the student is working but also direction about relevant theoretical literature from other disciplines. As students reflect upon whether certain pieces of literature are directly relevant to the focus of their research, it is important to have a clear mind of what the research questions are as a reminder to ask themselves whether each piece of literature should be included. It is generally assumed that supervisors should have a relatively wide knowledge of the literature relevant to their students' researches and that they can identify gaps in their students' selection of content and direct them to literature they believe they should consider including.

The amount of literature

Literature reviews can easily become too expansive. More often than not, the amount of detail given on the empirical literature will be a key reason for this. Some students think that they need to present information on every component of a published study rather than select only that which directly relates to the key idea they are writing about. Another issue concerning the amount of literature selected is how up-to-date it needs to be. It sometimes needs to be pointed out to students that some of their older literature can be summarized or just referenced with other literature if more recent publications have drawn on or referred to the older literature. As a rough guide to the size of the literature review, it should not exceed a third the length of the whole writing.

Critical engagement with the literature

Critical questions should be thought. To what extent are the conclusions that an author makes based on the findings that have been reported Are the findings informed by a sound and robust research methodology? Students need to critically assess the literature informing the claims of a theoretical position and point out the value and credibility of the literature before making their own stand. As support for both theoretically based and empirically based claims, students often make quite extensive use of citations, but they are not always used effectively for the purpose of arguing or justifying their choice. Many universities provide seminars and workshops on critically assessing or evaluating literature, so students are recommended to join such sessions to get specific instructions.

7.4.3 The Methodology Chapter

Students begin thinking about the methodology they will use to investigate their research questions while reading the literature for their initial and confirmed proposals. While feedback may have been given on these documents, it is not until they are required to write up a first full version of their methodology chapter that other issues may emerge. The first version of the methodology chapter needs to be completed before students start their research if they are to be sure that additional options will not emerge once the research has commenced. Students want to start their data collection as soon as they finish the writing of literature review, but they need to complete a detailed full version of their methodology chapter first, to prevent any flaws in the design of methodology.

Areas covered in the chapter

The necessary areas needed to be identified in this chapter include, for example, credibility (validity and reliability) which is one area that is frequently not included. Another area is a philosophical explanation and justification of the methodological approach considered relevant to the focus of their study. While students typically have no difficulty commenting and justifying the qualitative, quantitative or mixed methods approaches of their planned research, they often don't realize the need to justify these approaches with a discussion of the philosophical approach that is relevant to the aims of the research and therefore to reasons why a qualitative, quantitative or mixed methods approach is appropriate. It is important to notify these explanations and justifications.

Insufficient detail for a replication of the research

There are frequently gaps in the information provided in this chapter on processes and procedures. While students often know in great detail what they did when conducting their research, they often fail to report all of the steps and procedures. Readers of the chapter need to be able to replicate their study if they want to, using the detail presented and that, if they are unable to progress from one stage to another, it is likely to be because they have not been given sufficiently detailed information. An example of this problem can be seen in Box 7.8 below where a small excerpt from the data analysis section of a methodology chapter is presented. It can be seen that readers who want to replicate this type of analysis may have difficulty doing so given the lack of detail with regard to what obligatory occasion analysis is and how it is applied to the student's data, what the revised version of the index of accuracy included and what "overuse" is.

> **Box 7.8 An Example of Insufficient Methodological Detail**
>
> An index of accuracy (obligatory occasion analysis with consideration of over- use) was

calculated based on similar calculations used in previous research. In two studies (Shintani & Ellis, 2013; Shintani, Ellis & Suzuki, 2014) where there was a possibility to overuse the target feature, a revised version of this index of accuracy was adopted with consideration being given to overuse. As there are possibilities to overuse both of the target features in this study, the same revised version of obligatory occasion analysis was adopted.

Unclear alignment Between research questions and data sources

Because the research questions are likely to be presented in a different section of the chapter to the data source information (i.e. instruments), there is a need to connect these two. For instance, it may not be clear how one of the research questions was investigated (i.e. what data sources provided the data for answering the question). One approach that can be effective for addressing this problem is to create a table with column one stating the research questions and column two stating the data sources. Doing this makes it immediately clear if additional sources need to be considered. Once this alignment has been addressed, a third column can be created between the first column and the second so they can define in detail key words, constructs and terms referred to in the research questions. This exercise will often reveal a number of matters that the student has not fully considered. For example, they may not have considered how their data sources are going to provide information for all aspects of each research question. This practice helps to write this part of the chapter more clearly. An example of this approach is provided in Table 7.8.

Table 7.8 An Example of Alignment

Research questions	Definitions	Data sources
1. How do Chinese EFL teachers make their decisions about what to write and how to write it when giving EFL students feedback on their writing?	EFL = English as a foreign language Feedback = written comment on any aspect of the writing	Background interview; think-aloud protocol; retrospective interview
2. How effective is the communication between the teacher and the student as a result of the feedback?	Communication effectiveness = understanding by the student of what is intended by the teacher	On-going and final interviews; students' writing; student feedback and self-evaluation

7.4.4 The Findings Chapter

Placement of Explanation and Discussion of Finding

If students are presenting their findings in a separate chapter to the discussion of their findings, they need to be clear that an identification and an explanation of a finding should appear in the findings chapter, and that a discussion of the explanation should be left to the discussion chapter. Sometimes, it is easier for readers to navigate their way through a large number of findings and discussion points if these are presented together for each research question. For example, the findings of research question 1 could be immediately followed by the discussion of these findings before the findings and discussion of research question 2 are presented. If this approach is adopted, it may be that more than one chapter is considered desirable. For instance, research questions relating to a particular theme may be presented together in one chapter while research questions relating to another theme may be presented in another chapter. So, putting findings in one separate part and discussion of findings in another paragraph is a reasonable approach.

Organization of Findings

The manner in which the findings are presented needs to be logical and consistent. One form of logic typically chosen is that which presents the findings in the same order in which they are referred to in earlier chapters. For example, in some disciplines, the research questions are stated in the introduction chapter and/or in the literature review chapter(s) and there is usually a logic to how they are sequenced. Readers find it helpful if there is a consistency of approach across chapters, especially if the findings are presented according to the listed sequence and the same sequence is followed in the discussion chapter.

Another organizational approach that will help readers navigate their way through the findings of a specific research question and understand their relative importance or significance to the question is one which presents the most important findings first.

Tables and Figures

Tables and figures are frequently presented in a findings chapter to show the relationship of items in a table and to visually represent the tabled items in a figure. While most students are able to create tables and figures without difficulty, they may not fully get the fact that the reader of their work does not have the knowledge that they have to understand detailed and/or complex tables and figures. Students will sometimes provide very little textual commentary to assist the reader's understanding of a table or figure. They may provide, for example, an introductory comment on what statistics in a table show but not add further detail to explain what they want their readers to focus on and in what order. The example of good practice presented in Box 7.9 below introduces the topic and focus of the table before inserting the table itself. This is then followed up with a textual commentary on what the student wants the reader to understand.

Box 7.9 An Example of Table Presentation and Commentary

Table 7.9 shows the descriptive statistics for the accuracy scores in using the passive voice in the writing tasks. It indicates that the accuracy of all the three groups (DCF, ME and WP) kept improving overtime, and that the improvement is greater for the DCF group than the WP group. The somewhat high deviation in each group indicates wide variability within groups, which may limit the ability to find significance.

Table 7.9 Descriptive Statistics for the Scores of Accuracy in Using the Passive Voice

Group	N	Time 1		Time 2		Time 3	
		Mean	SD	Mean	SD	Mean	SD
DCF	29	37.75	30.88	48.91	31.09	54.44	33.78
ME	30	37.43	27.68	53.91	31.93	65.70	27.57

A mixed ANOVA found a significant main effect of time averaging across the groups ($F (2, 168) = 11.39$, $p < .001$, $\eta 2 = .12$), but no significant main effect of group collapsing across time ($F (2, 84) = 1.26$, $p = .29$, $\eta 2 = .03$). Further comparison between pairs of time points indicate participants demonstrate a significant improvement in accuracy from Time 1 to Time 2 ($F (1, 84) = 6.71$, $p = .01$, $\eta 2 = .07$), from Time 2 to Time 3 ($F (1, 84) = 4.28$, $p = .04$, $\eta 2 = .05$), and from Time 1 to Time 3 ($F (1, 84) = 25.01$, $p=.001$, $\eta 2 = .23$). These indicate that all the treatment types (DCF, ME and WP) contributed to the improvement in accuracy overtime, and this is in accordance with the results of descriptive analyses reported above. The mixed ANOVA also reveals there was no significant time and group interaction ($F (4, 168) = 1.02$, $p = .40$, $\eta 2 = .02$), which indicates there were no significant differences in the patterns of improvement amongst the groups. In other words, no treatment type is significantly more effective than the others in producing improved accuracy in the use of the passive voice.

Format

Sometimes students are inconsistent in the formatting of their findings. Feedback may need to draw their attention to the conventions typically used in their discipline. For example, if APA (American Psychological Association) conventions are used in the list of references, APA conventions also need to be used consistently throughout the formatting of the dissertation.

7.4.5 The Discussion Chapter

When writing the discussion chapter, the following two aspects are needed to be considered. What should the discussion points be? Whet is to the effectiveness of the links between the discussion peints and the wider field of knowledge?

The Points of Discussion

For consistency and ease of reading, the discussion of findings needs to be set out logically and, as far as possible, structured according to the way in which the findings have been presented. Refer to the previous section on the presentation of findings where it was explained that the discussion points on each research question might follow the presentation of each finding. or be presented in a separate discussion chapter. Sometimes, discussion chapter is mingled together with the conclusion. However, some students may choose to provide this as a separate discussion of findings chapter.

Linking the Findings to the Wider Literature

There are frequently issues with the discussion of findings in light of the literature, that is, the wider picture that has been presented in the literature review. Students will often discuss the extent to which a finding corroborates or contradicts the findings of other studies, but the reader may be left to ponder "so what?" Feedback, in this situation, would do well to suggest that the student also

(a) consider the theoretical literature in order to explain what the reader can understand to have been the reason for any corroboration or contradiction and (b) reflect upon the methodology used in his/her study, and that of the other studies, to see if an explanation can then be offered to explain the similarity and/or difference in findings. Additionally, supervisors may want to draw their students' attention to ways in which examples from the data may explain the findings. Having discussed each separate finding, they should ask themselves whether or not a claim can be made on the basis of their discussion points and/or whether a conclusion can be drawn.

7.4.6 The Conclusion Chapter

Many of the typical sections of a conclusion chapter are handled fairly well by students but, within each section, there may be issues that need to be suggested.

A Reader–friendly Summary of Findings

The conclusion will typically start with a brief overview of the aims of the study and the methodological approach that was employed in order to frame what is said in the chapter. This is usually followed by a summary of the findings of the study. While the findings may have been summarized at various places in the findings chapter, they are often summarized in the presentation of findings chapter in terms of the type of analysis that was undertaken. In the conclusion chapter, the preferred version is to summarize the findings for a non-expert, layman's understanding, so that an intelligent non-specialist can understand them.

Making Claims and Drawing Conclusions

The conclusion chapter is all about making claims and drawing conclusions. It is suggested that the strength of claims and conclusions should be emphasized. Students are not very confident with their findings and need encouragement to say that a new finding or a particularly significant finding has been revealed in their research. In all situations, clear evidence and an appropriate strength of assertion is necessary. However, students often need feedback on what can be said and how it can be said. Cooley and Lewkowicz (2003) offered excellent guidelines on how to write claims and conclusions that can be found.

Limitations

A consideration of the limitations of the student's study should include the following two points. One is the limitation in terms of any weaknesses or flaws that they have become aware of during their practice and the ether is the limitation in terms of the scope or parameters of the research project. Students are sometimes reluctant to be totally point out weaknesses or flaws in particular but it needs to be explained to them that they will be seen as more ready to do independent research if they can identify these and show that they understand the extent to which they may have negatively impacted on their findings.

Further Research

Recommendations for further research often arise out of the identified limitations but students often fail to connect their limitations with recommended further research directions. If this is the case, it is useful for students to create a table with two columns and to identify the limitations in column one and consider whether in column two there might be suggestions that can be offered for further research.

The Contribution to the Field

This section, which typically comes after the summary of findings, is arguably the most important part of the dissertation because it provides the student with an opportunity to show that they understand the importance and significance of their work for the field in which it was situated. However, it can very often be a section that presents a rather superficial "discussion" and that focuses mainly on the contribution to empirical knowledge. The suggestions needed to be signaled out are as follows. One is to focus students' attention on any aspects of their research focus that were not well investigated and therefore not well answered (e.g. as a result of methodological shortcomings). The next is to recommend replications or that further related studies adopt certain additional approaches.

7.4.7 The Abstract

Hyland (2000) refers to research that identified various discourse content unit preferences found in the abstracts of different disciplines. While prewriting advice should focus on what the supervisor and student consider relevant and important for the student's abstract, written feedback will often require suggestions about where more or less could be said about a particular discourse content units. Hyland's book will be very helpful for students if they need more direction in drafting their abstracts. Having considered the advice and the feedback in that book, students can get detailed advice on their selection of content and on what advice and feedback may need to be provided on how the content is used in the creation of argument.

Chapter 8
Argument in Academic Writing

In writings like the academic articles, the content is organized as an "argument" that, in one way or another, explains and develops rhetorically a case to support and justify the inclusion of the selected content. As the previous chapters explained, the nature of the content, and the argument it serves, vary from one chapter to another. Thus, the argument of a literature review, for example, is different to the argument of a results chapter. Once students and supervisors have a clear understanding of the relevant content and how it can be most effectively organized, they need to understand that the argument is only going to be rhetorically effective if there is a coherent logic to the way the content is presented. The aim of this chapter, then, is to present some prewriting advice to help students to write a successful argument.

8.1 Academic Writing Argument

In academic writing, the term "argument" can refer to a proposition that is supported with evidence or reasoning. It is "a connected series of statements intended to establish a position and implies a response to another (or more than one) position" (Andrews, 1995, p. 3) or to "a sequence of interlinked claims and reasons that, between them, establish content and force of the position for which a particular speaker/writer is arguing" (Toulmin, Reike, & Janik, 1984, p. 14). Thus, the first defining characteristic of an argument is the development of a position. The second feature is a presentation of the position through the logical sequence of propositions that establish the position. The third characteristic of an argument is the selection of relevant information for supporting the development of the position.

8.2 Different Argument Structures of Academic Article Chapters

8.2.1 The Introduction Chapter Argument

It is often a good idea to brief students about the introductory nature of this chapter. A number of important issues may need to be mentioned.

Define Terms and Concepts

Sometimes too much details are provided when defining terms or concepts that are referred to in dissertation. In these situations, only a clear and simple, layman's type of definition at this stage is needed but which refers the reader to the literature review chapter where a more detailed discussion of terms and concepts presented. For instance, when researching the role of various factors in the learning of a second language (L2), researchers will need to explain what they mean by terms such as "L2 development", "L2 acquisition" and "L2 learning". In the introduction chapter, it is better to provide a simple definition of these terms and leave the wider discussion of the differences between each of them to the literature review chapter where there is space for a detailed explanation of differences as are revealed in the published literature. As well as providing a simple working definition of terms and constructs, readers may also need to know if there are certain constraints or parameters that concern the research. For instance, the research may be more about one stage of cognitive processing, so in this situation that stage should be explained more fully than the other stages even though the other stages will need to be explained in order to provide sufficient information for the reader.

Literature Detail

The discussion of literatures needs to be focused on what is necessary background for the research questions. Providing the type of overview that readers need in the opening chapter can best be achieved once the literature review chapter has been completed. Often, early drafts of the introduction chapter will provide about different theories that are considered relevant to the research question of the study and fail to explain the connection between the theories and research questions. In other words, there may be an absent explanation about what the literature explains and predicts about the findings of the study.

Overview of the Paper

An overview of the structure of the paper is not difficult to write but many students provide little more than a "shopping list" of what will be covered in each chapter. In doing so, they miss an opportunity to argue why and how the material they refer to is important. That is to say, what the argument will focus on and why the reader needs to know this information need to be reinforced.

8.2.2 The literature review argument

For a literature review, it is very likely to include more than one claim or proposition about the wider knowledge territory relevant to the focus of their dissertation. A mind-map shows the relationship between key sections or topics of the literature review and the various claims or propositions about each section/topic, and hence establishes a general argument for their literature review. Once claims or propositions about an area of content knowledge have been described, explained and criticized, gaps in the area of knowledge can be identified and discussed. Having done this for one key area or section of content, the process can be repeated for all the sections. Once these have been presented and the gaps have been identified, the announcement of how the research gap can be occupied will be presented. From these, the research questions/hypotheses can be formulated.

Usually, the literature review argument is the most difficult to write because of the amount of information that needs to be included and the complexity involved in structuring an argument. It is likely that more iterations of this chapter's argument will be required than for those of other chapters of the dissertation. Even when clear advice is given, many will struggle with the level of skill required to create a clear, logical, and rhetorically effective argument from beginning to end. So, the following are some of the key areas of suggestions needed to be provided.

List Topic Related to the Research

There is a tendency for students to present a range of literature-informed sections in the first draft of their literature review that one might typically find in a book that surveys key topics related to the field. In such volumes, the topics are usually listed in some logical sequence (e.g. they might be presented according to a chronological order, thematic order or general-to-specific order, etc.). However, the literature review needs to be organized in such a way that it relates directly to the main argument. Thus, attention needs to be drawn to argue why and how the literature, that has been selected, is relevant to the academic article and ensure that one proposition/claim/argument leads to and informs the next.

Evaluate Literature Critically

It is difficult to critically assess the quality of different claims and conclusions reported in the literature, and the validity, reliability of empirical research and the claims/conclusions it has led to. Many literature reviews will simply provide a descriptive outline of different theoretical positions and different research findings or use them for the purposes of arguing a proposition instead of critically evaluating them. When discussing various theoretical perspectives that are potentially relevant to the focus of the dissertation research, students need to identify these perspectives and explain why they have situated their research focus within only one or some of these. Additionally, the closely related theoretical literatures need to be selective in order to picture the potential relevance of other theoretical meanings.

8.2.3 The Methodology Chapter Argument

While the methodology chapter usually presents the methods, processes or theories by which the research is done, argumentative writing is still a possibility in this chapter. Hence, there is a necessity to discuss the argument structure of this chapter.

The "Why" as Well as the "What"

Each aspect of an academic writing requires a consideration of "why". The justification of the choice of methodologies may need to be provided in certain parts of the chapter. The explanation of why one of two equally relevant approaches was adopted in the methodology and why the second of the two was not selected is needed in methodology part (e.g. why interviews were included instead of survey questionnaires). Students need to consider the instrument best able to provide the data that are relevant to the central focus of a research question. Thus, students may need to have their attention drawn to the importance of justifying their descriptive "what" details in the argument structure of the chapter. Then, the "why" component of the argument must be presented to point out that the justification of the methodology chosen which is well related to the "what" component. So this chapter needs to describe in careful detail the various component parts of the framework, it also needs to explain what these parts contribute to the analysis and why.

Procedural Gaps in the Argument

It is very easy for students to know the detail about the processes and procedures they included in their methodology, but even easier for them to forget to mention a critical procedure that enabled them to move from one step to another. Another part of the methodology chapter which may need to provide suggestion on is the data collection process. This is particularly important if data have been collected from a range of sources and instruments at different times. Suggesting that all this information in a table that identifies the sequence of each step in the collection process is presented is one effective way of helping to eliminate the omission of key information. Once the table having been created, the accompanying text is likely to be more complete.

8.2.4 The Result Chapter Argument

Distinguish Between an Explanation and a Discussion

Sometimes, an explanation about what a group of findings means and what the numbers in a table mean, may suddenly become a point of discussion. If the presentation and discussion of findings is being presented in the same chapter, this is not an issue. It is easy to confuse the two words "explanation" and "discussion". For instance, pointing to patterns in the findings of a research question is not a discussion. Explaining why the patterns occurred as they did would be a discussion of possible reasons.

Layman's Explanation Versus Technical Explanation

Typically, a presentation of findings involves the use of technical terms associated with the analysis process. This is not a problem, but students sometimes need to be reminded that, at the end of each finding, it is expected that there will be an explanation of the finding in layman's terms, so it is clear what it reveals about one of the research questions. Sometimes students have difficulty making this transition because they have become so immersed in the analytical process that they struggle to explain the finding in terms that an non-expert will understand. This final step in the presentation of a finding is an important component of the argument structure of the chapter and examiners will want to see that students are able to explain their work with and without technical terminology.

8.2.5 The Discussion Chapter Argument

Like the argument structure of the literature review chapter, the argument of the discussion of results chapter can also be challengeable.

Provide Thorough Discussion

A finding may not warrant an extensive discussion. In several respects, students may fail to take the discussion of their findings as far as they can. For example, they may only give a partial explanation for why a finding occurred as it did (i.e. whether it met expectations). Feedback may need to consider more fully the reasons for a particular finding occurring as it did (e.g. by comparing the methodology of their study with those of other studies where differences in variables may have been a primary reason for any difference in findings). Additionally, students are sometimes satisfied if they can suggest one explanation for a finding and may need to be prompted to consider the influence or interacting effect of other factors or variables. Then, at the end of their discussion, there may be an opportunity for them to make a claim or draw a conclusion about the finding that they have been discussed. It may also be necessary to draw their attention to this additional point of discussion.

Offer Wider Perspective

The argument in the discussion chapter needs to be developed so that it is clear what the findings have contributed to the wider field of knowledge. It is this aspect of the discussion that are seldom engaged with, because the findings may be felt too limited in scope to have a significant impact beyond the scopes of study. Explaining the connection between one's own findings and the knowledge already established in the field is arguably the most important part of any discussion of findings.

8.2.6 The Conclusion Chapter Argument

Summary of Findings

Because the conclusion chapter is sometimes read before other chapters, the summary of findings needs to be written in non-technical language and be directly explained in terms of the aims or research questions/hypotheses in clarity and explicitness.

Contribution to the Field of Knowledge

In many respects, this is the most important part of the dissertation because it shows an understanding of what it adds to the body of knowledge. The argument it presents, in this regard, needs to be carefully organized and carefully explained/justified. In particular, while students can usually see clearly and explain clearly what their findings have contributed as new empirical knowledge, they sometimes struggle to use this as a platform from which to argue their contribution to theory-building. Having argued the contribution to the areas, it is not difficult to suggest a range of practice applications. However, the suggestions which are outside the scope of the study or have not been specifically derived from the findings of the study should be avoided.

Limitations

Limitations can refer to the scope or parameters of a study as well as to any weaknesses or shortcomings in a study. Students usually understand the need to refer to the latter even though they may be reluctant to identify too many of these in case they may undermine what they have said about the contribution of their work to the field. The results of research may not be compromised with limitations.

8.2.7 The Abstract Argument

Equivalence Between Aims/Research Questions and Range of Findings.

If there are a number of supporting or operational research questions, for example, these may need to be reduced to two or three of the main aims/research questions. This, in turn, may mean that the range of findings identified in the abstract should echo the number of research aims/questions and that the inclusion of those findings should directly align with the aims/questions that have been identified. Make sure that no new findings are stated out of the range of research questions.

Chapter 9
Composing Methods for Academic Writing

To help you understand what content and structure is appropriate for the different parts of your thesis, the chapter presents a range of options, illustrating them with analyses of well-written theses in Applied Linguistics. Examining the discourse genre enables us to understand the type of content that is typically presented with rhetorical effectiveness. The term "genre" has been defined in a variety of ways but, its first characteristic is that a genre is a type of discourse that occurs in a particular setting. In this case, the particular setting is an academic setting which is defined by the academic community of researchers, teachers, examiners, supervisors and institutions. The second characteristic is that a genre has distinctive and recognizable patterns and norms with respect to content and structure. In other words, the type of content and structure that you observe in one thesis will be obviously similar to that observed in other theses. Therefore, each of the section in this chapter will focus on a different part-genre and each will begin with an outline of its purpose and functions as mentioned in Chapter 7, followed by a consideration of the type of content that might be presented and, in doing so, they will be illustrated with extracts from the sample theses. It will be emphasized throughout the chapter that the purpose and functions presented in each section are options and you do not need to feel constrained by the range presented. Depending on the topic and focus of your thesis, you may be able to add more content.

The chapter comprises eight sections with each being devoted to a part of the thesis. The structure of each section is mostly like this. After an introduction, there will be the purpose and functions of the part of the thesis, which is followed by an outline of the content units that can be employed in the presentation of content. The extent to which these units and sub-units are employed and the way in which they are organized is then illustrated from the sample theses. Following this material, answers to frequently asked questions are provided.

Throughout the chapter, illustrations will be drawn from one sample thesis. For the sake of clarity, to select one that was well written and that illustrated many of the features typically found in empirical theses will be a reasonable way to provide a model. Then it is easy to apply what learned to other texts and theses. It will help to decide what to include in the thesis and how to present materials in an effective manner. This chapter is a reference guide to write various parts of the thesis. Both the instructions and analysis of the materials can be presented to guide students' writing.

9.1 Thesis Introduction

In this section, we will be considering the opening chapter of a thesis. First, we will reflect on its purpose or functions and then look at the type of content that is typically presented and at ways in which it might be organized. Having considered these options, we will then analyze the extent to which the introductory chapter of our sample thesis used these options. This analysis will lead on to a discussion of some of the linguistic features that are characteristic of introductory chapters.

9.1.1 The Functions of a Thesis Introduction

As mentioned in Chapter 7 (Bitchener, 2018), the primary purpose of the introductory chapter is to inform the reader to the thesis. Most often, this will involve the following contents.

(1) A description of the problem.
(2) A review of the background and of what is known.
(3) An identification of gaps of knowledge.
(4) An explanation of what you plan to do to address these gaps.
(5) An explanation of the contribution of the thesis.
(6) An outline of the structure of the thesis.

Although it is not necessary to cover all of these contents, at least the consideration of each one is essential. In the following section, we will look at how these functions might be achieved in the opening chapter.

9.1.2 The Content and Structure of a Thesis Introduction

As we have seen in Chapter 7 of this book, researchers have analyzed the typical content and organizational patterns of different parts of a thesis and produced frameworks of what they have found. Quite a lot of attention has been given to the introductory chapter of theses and the corresponding section of research articles. The discourse content unit options in the following table (ahich has been introduced in Chapter 7) may be a guidance for the selection of content of the chapter. The sub-units indicate how the three main units may be discussed (Bitchener, 2018).

These are presented as options rather than requirements. In the analysis of the sample introductory chapter, we will see the extent to which the author has utilized each of these content units. Every approach can be equally valid and effective in terms of introducing the reader to the thesis.

Main units	Sub-units
1. Establish a research territory.	a. Explain the extent to which it is important, central, interesting, problematic or relevant.
	b. Provide background information about the area.
	c. Introduce and review aspects of previous literature in the area (theoretical, empirical and non-research literature).
	d. Define terms and constructs on first mention.
2. Establish a research gap in the territory.	a. Indicate a gap in the literature.
	b. Raise a question about a gap in the literature.
	c. Identify a problem or need.
	d. Extend previous knowledge.
3. Occupy the research gap.	a. Outline the purpose, aim, objectives of the research study.
	b. Specify the research questions, hypotheses that were investigated.
	c. Outline the relevant theoretical frameworks, perspectives, positions.
	d. Describe the methodology/design of the study.
	e. Indicate the scope and parameters of the study.
	f. Explain the likely contribution and value of the research to the field of knowledge.
	g. Outline the chapter organization of the study.

9.1.3 Analysis of a Sample Thesis

In this section, we will analyze and discuss the content units used by the author of a master's introductory chapter. The master's thesis is entitled *Willingness to Communicate in a Second Language Classroom*. The thesis investigates the willingness of second language learners of English to communicate in a second language learning classroom.

It examines whether their willingness to take part in interactive activities is determined by innate trait-like factors and/or situation-specific factors, including participation in pair work, small group interactions and plenary discussions Try to identify which options have been used in the introduction section. With the main and sub units presented above.

1) Background of the Study

In this section, we focus our attention on the background information section of the thesis introduction.

For many learners, the ultimate goal of language learning is to use the language for authentic and effective communication in everyday life. This conforms to the concept of communicative language teaching (CLT), a dominant feature of modern language pedagogy, which places its major emphasis on learning through communication (Ellis, 2004). Long's (1996) update of the Interaction Hypothesis has suggested that second language interaction provides learners with opportunities to receive comprehensible input, to produce and modify their output, to test out hypotheses and to notice gaps existing in their interlanguage, which in turn, can facilitate language development (Mackey, 2002, p. 380).	Background information

It has been argued by some researchers (for example, Skehan, 1989) that language is best learnt through communication, a notion stressing that learners have to talk in order to learn (Skehan 1989, p. 48). Swain's (1985, 1995) Output Hypothesis suggested that output serves as oral practice by providing opportunities for learners to test hypotheses about the rules they have constructed for the target language. At the same time, this may lead to greater meta-linguistic awareness so that learners may pay particular attention to form. This may in turn cause them to "notice a gap between what they want to say and what they can say, leading them to recognize what they do not know, or know only partially" (Swain, 1995, p. p. 125~126) in the process of struggling to produce output comprehensible to their interlocutors (Mackey, 2002).	Background information
In the last decade, there has been a growing body of research that has had its focus on an individual difference variable — willingness to communicate (WTC) — a non-linguistic construct that would seem to be of obvious interest in the area of communicative language teaching (Ellis 2004). Some researchers — for example, MacIntyre, Clement, DÖrnyei and Noels, 1998; MacIntyre, Baker, Clement and Donovan,	Centrality, background, and previous research
2003— have advocated that a fundamental goal of second language education should be the creation of willingness to communicate in the language learning process, in order to produce students who are willing to seek out communication opportunities and to use the language for authentic communication. MacIntyre, Baker, Clement and Conrod (2001) have argued that WTC should be expected to facilitate the language learning process, a view based on their finding that higher WTC among students translates into increased opportunity for practice in an L2 and authentic L2 usage.	
A widely accepted definition of WTC in L2 was suggested by MacIntyre et al. (1998, p. 547), who considered this construct as a readiness to enter into discourse at a particular time with a specific person or persons using an L2. Specific to an L2 classroom, WTC was defined by Oxford (1997, p. 449) as "a student's intention to interact with others in the target language, given a chance to do so". Both definitions emphasized that one would have the freedom to decide whether to communicate or not in a particular context. Also, both definitions treated WTC in a very broad sense, which included its applications to both written and spoken communication. In their study, MacIntyre et al. (2001) examined WTC in four macro skills of speaking, listening, reading and writing, both inside and outside the classroom. Given the scope of this present study, WTC will be considered only in terms of spoken communication within an L2 classroom.	Definitions Previous research and the scope of research

Paragraphs 1~2: In the first 7 sentences, background information about the wider research territory is provided. Essentially, these sentences are introducing us to the theoretical framework of the study. The key theorists have to say about the aim of second language learning and how they believe it occurs. In this way, the specific theoretical focus of the research is placed: the contribution of one variable (a learner's willingness to communicate in a language learning classroom) to the learning process.

Paragraph 3: These sentences of paragraph 3, introduce us three points. The first is the centrality and importance of the specific areas of research within the wider context. The second is a willingness to communicate that is an essential part of the language learning process. The third is one empirical research that supports the relationship between a willingness to communicate and taking opportunities to communicate in the second language.

Paragraph 4: In this paragraph, the willingness to communicate construct is defined. A broad definition is provided before a specific definition related to second language classrooms is given. The focus of one earlier study on willingness to communicate in four macro skills is then introduced. The final sentence in this section announces the scope of the study to be reported in the following chapters of the thesis — an investigation of a learner's willingness to communicate orally. Thus, the scope of the thesis has been announced as a lead-in to the following section on the specific aims of the research.

2) Aims of the Research

1. The primary purpose of the study is to explore the dual characteristics of the willingness to communicate construct, following the trait/state dichotomy claimed by some researchers; that is, it aims to examine whether the willingness to communicate construct operates at the trait level or at the state level. The study also aims to investigate how the construct operates in three interactional contexts in a second language classroom: whole class, small groups and dyads.	Aims
2. The study involved eight international students enrolled in a general English program at a language school in Auckland. Their self-report WTC was identified by means of a WTC questionnaire at the beginning of the program. Then, during the entire span of the program, the learners' WTC behavior in a whole class situation was observed and recorded on a classroom observation scheme. WTC behavior in groups and dyads was also examined in terms of the students' task performance in group and pair work, which was audio-taped and coded on the classroom observation scheme subsequently. Factors that learners perceived as being most important in determining their WTC in class were explored through interviews with volunteer participants.	Method and scope
3. In general, the current study has employed a multiple research approach in order to provide a more holistic and comprehensive view of the WTC construct in second language learning.	Method

4. This study contributes to an understanding of the role played by WTC in second language instruction, through an exploration of how WTC operates in a second language classroom. While a number	Contribution
of studies related to the present research have been undertaken in the past (see MacIntyre et al. 2001, 2003; Yashima et al, 2002, 2004), the focus of this earlier work was based predominantly on self-report, rather than actual classroom behavior. Arguably, there remains a need to incorporate a qualitative approach to examine WTC, in order to verify antecedents affecting WTC through behavioral studies of the L2 classroom. The dynamic aspect of WTC — that is to say, how WTC varies overtime — was largely ignored in previous studies. This present study differs from these to the extent that it provides more comprehensive evidence covering both WTC based on a self-report questionnaire and WTC in actual behavior, as well as the dynamics of the WTC construct. The results of this study may therefore be of benefit in second language instruction if they convince instructors of the importance of creating WTC among learners in the L2 classroom.	Gap Need Gap Aim and Contribution Contribution

Paragraph 5: This section of the introduction chapter begins with an announcement of the two key aims of the study. The author has indirectly established the claim by some researchers and that, by implication, it needs to be investigated and resolved. Later in this paragraph, you will see that a more explicit announcement of the gap is provided.

Paragraph 6: Having announced the aims of the research, the author proceeds to explain its scope and describes some key elements of the methodology that were employed. The following sentences explain that only eight international students took part in the study and that they were enrolled in a general English program at a language school in Auckland, New Zealand, and the specific methods to collect the research databy questionnaire, observation scheme, audio-taping and interviews.

Paragraph 7: This paragraph is a single sentence which continues with a statement about the overall methodological approach of the study and a justification for this approach.

Paragraph 8: In this paragraph, the author explains the aim of the research and its contribution to the wider field of knowledge and in doing so, relates it to several statements about the need for the investigation. The author explains that the study contributes to the understanding we already have of the role played by a learner's willingness to contribute in the second language learning process. A second gap in the existing research is stated. Having identified areas in which further research is needed, the author proceeds to state how the research has filled that gap or need. At last, the section was concluded with a contribution to how the findings from the study could be applied in the second language classroom.

This section introduces us to the aims of the study before the research gap is explicitly stated.

Explicit references to the gaps are integrated into the contributions of present study. As such, they have been introduced in the context of how previous research will be developed as a result of the focus of this study. The recycling of gaps/needs with contributions is very prevailing phenomenon in this aim section, which pave a solid foundation for the clear statement of the purpose of the study.

3) Organization of the Study

This section of the introductory chapter provides an overview of how the remaining chapters of the thesis have been organized. In many respects, it is like an expanded version of a table of contents. In a sense, the paragraph structure of this section follows the structural outline of the abstract. In short, it tells the reader how the thesis is organized and why it is done in this way.

9. This thesis consists of six chapters. Following this introduction, Chapter 2 reviews extant literature and research that motivates and generates the research questions addressed in this thesis. It also considers, from a variety of perspectives, how WTC research represents a new trend in motivational research and reviews some major findings from empirical research studies concerning WTC in LI, L2, L3, and L4. Gaps in previous research are subsequently identified and the research questions are raised for investigation. 10. Chapter 3 depicts the methodological approach adopted in the study. In order to enrich the data from different perspectives, a multi-method design was adopted; justification for this approach is provided. It is contended that such a research design is advantageous to the extent that it offers the possibility of providing results that complement, elaborate and confirm each other. The major research instruments — the Willingness to Communicate, survey, a classroom observation scheme, and structured interviews, are identified and the procedures followed in collecting and analyzing data are stated. 11. Key findings from an analysis of the research data are presented in Chapter 4. These include results based on the use of both qualitative and quantitative research techniques. Results from a content analysis of the interview data are also considered. 12. Chapter 5 includes a detailed account and interpretation of the findings of the study, with reference to each of the research questions and in relation to previous relevant research findings. 13. Chapter 6 summarizes the study findings, focuses on both pedagogical and research implications of the study, and indicates its limitations.	Thesis outline

Paragraph 9: The first sentence states that the thesis is made up of 6 chapters. Then, Chapter 2 will consider the importance and significance of the study, together with a review of the published research literature on the willingness to communicate construct in both first and second language contexts. Finally, Chapter 2 will conclude with a statement where gaps in previous research lie and an announcement on which of these, stated as research questions, were investigated in the study.

Paragraph 10: The methodological approach of the thesis is outlined in this paragraph. Chapter 3 will introduce the methodology, a justification for the approach including its advantages, the data collection methods and how the data were collected and analyzed.

Paragraph 11: Chapter 4 will present both qualitative and quantitative findings. In writing this part of the chapter you need to make a number of judgments calls on what level of detail to include and what not to include.

Paragraph 12: Chapter 5 will be concerned with discussing the research findings of the study, using the findings to answer the research questions and discussing their significance and contribution to the big picture presented in Chapter 2.

Paragraph 13: This introductory chapter concludes with an outline of what is discussed in the final chapter of the thesis. They are a summary of the study's findings, the pedagogical and research implications of the study and the limitations of the study. It may be more appropriate to discuss limitations after the findings have been summarized so that any caveats which are considered before recommendations are made about how the findings could be applied. Additionally, it might also be more logical to discuss future research ideas after the discussion of limitations.

The previous two sections have introduced us to the context in which the study was situated, the aims of the study and the contribution that the research is expected to make to a wider field of knowledge, so all that remains is for the reader to be introduced to the way in which the study will be reported in the thesis, which is the function of this section.

4) Some Key Linguistic Features of a Thesis Introduction

There are a number of linguistic features that are worth high-lighting about the writing of a thesis introduction. While they are characteristic of this chapter, they are also features that you need to be aware of when writing the other chapters of your thesis. Because we are focusing our attention on them here for the first time our discussion will be more extensive than that provided in other chapters of the book. The choice of voice, vocabulary and structures will be discussed.

Active Versus Passive Voice

Both the active and passive voices have been included in the sample introduction. There is no hard and fast rule on this. It is a matter of whether or not you, as author, wish to give prominence at the beginning of a sentence to the object of the sentence rather than the subject (Bunton, 2002). If this is the case, authors will use the present perfect tense rather than the present tense. In some situations, if the author does not want to reveal the subject of a sentence, she/he will tend to use the passive voice. On other occasions, authors may want to make a stronger statement or suggest that something is an established fact, so they will make use of the passive voice. In our sample introduction, you can see, in the following sentences, that the author has made quite extensive use of the passive voice. In each case, it is likely that she wanted to give focus to the object of the sentence.

e.g. *Gaps in previous research are subsequently identified and the research questions are raised for investigation.*

e.g. *It is contended that such a research design is advantageous...*

Adjectives

Adjectives are used in order to emphasize the importance or centrality of the research territory and research focus of the study to be reported (Evans & Gruba, 2002). You can see, for example, in sentence 2, through the use of the adjective "dominant", that the focus on a communicative use of language in language learning classes has been central to research in the field. Compared with other theses that often include adjectives like "unique", "important" or "significant", this introductory chapter is more reserved in the way.

First Person Pronouns

Opinions vary about whether to use the first-person pronouns "I" and "we" in academic texts like the thesis. Some disciplines/departments/schools or individual supervisors believe that the use of the first person is too personal for an objective piece of academic reporting. As we have seen above, one way of solving the issue is to make use of the passive voice. The question of whether or not to use the first-person pronoun will be what the author needs to decide when explaining to the reader how the following chapters of the thesis have been structured. The same decision needs to be made when summarizing or reviewing what has been presented in a previous section of the thesis.

Contrastive Vocabulary and Structures

When it comes to identifying the gap that your research occupies, several different approaches might be taken. One of the most common techniques used to signal a gap is the use of contrasting conjunctions and phrases. Another approach that is frequently used is to include negative words or phrases that in some way highlight the fact that while "x" may have been examined, "y" has not been investigated.

e.g. *While a number of studies related to the present research have been undertaken in the past... the focus of this earlier work was based predominantly on self-report, rather than actual classroom behavior.*

If you read other theses, you will see that an almost endless range of lexical and structural approaches can be used to signal the research gap. Swales and Feak(2004) present examples of some of this range.

1. Verbs

Disregard; fail to consider; ignore; is limited to; misinterpret; neglect to consider; overestimate; overlook; suffer from; underestimate

2. Adjectives

Controversial; incomplete; inconclusive; misguided; questionable; unconvincing; unsatisfactory

3. *Noun Phrases*

Little information, attention, work, data, research

Few studies, investigations, researchers, attempts

No studies, data, calculations

None of these studies, findings, calculations

4. *Passive Forms*

It remains clear that

It would be of interest to

9.2 Literature review

In this part, we will be considering the functions of the literature review chapter, how to go about deciding what content should be included and how to most effectively organize it. Often the first draft is written during the preparation of a thesis proposal. Thereafter, sections of the literature review will be revised with new material being added and with some existing material possibly being excluded. In order to understand what is involved in literature review, we need to consider first the various aims or functions of the literature review chapter.

9.2.1 The Functions of a Thesis Literature Review

Having introduced your reader to the issue, problem or question in the introduction chapter, the aim of the literature review is to provide an in-depth account of the background literature relevant to the context that your study is situated in and, in doing so, to provide an "argument" for the study. There are the following functions being presented in this chapter.

(1) A review of the research literature relevant to the study.

(2) A review of the theoretical perspectives that underpin or inform the research.

(3) An identification of arguments for and against issues and an identification of strengths and weaknesses of the value of relevant studies.

(4) An identification of gaps or shortcomings in this knowledge.

(5) A justification of why the gap is important and significant enough to be filled.

(6) An explanation of how the design of the research project was informed.

As you can see from this list of functions, they form a clear and logical outline for the literature review. These will help to determine the type of content that is relevant to the review and guide to most effectively organize it so that it reveals the "argument" underpinning the study.

9.2.2 The Content and Structure of a Thesis Literature Review.

The content of the review comprises a series of theme/topic units that review the non-research literature and research literature relevant to your research project. But, the review is more than just a summary of this material; it identifies gaps or shortcomings in the reported knowledge and research, and is also an explanation of why the gap that is addressed is important and significant enough to warrant the attention of study. Having done this, the final task in the review will be to announce how the research project sought to answer the research questions informed by the gap. According to this logic, the structure and content of literature review chapter can be shown in the following table (which has been introduced in Chapter 7) (Bitchener, 2018). Although some authors choose to signal how they will aim to address the issue(s) raised or how they will fill a particular knowledge gap during their presentation of a unit, others will discuss them at the end of the unit or in the concluding section of the literature review. So, the content and sequence of units and sub-units included in this chapter are optional for authors to choose.

Main units	Sub–units
1. Establish some aspect of the knowledge territory relevant to your research.	a. Present knowledge claims and statements about theories, beliefs, constructs and definitions.
	b. Explain the centrality, importance or significance of the area of knowledge.
	c. Present the research evidence (e. g. findings, methodology).
2. Create a research gap in knowledge.	a. Critique knowledge claims, issues, problems associated with Unit 1 claims, present research evidence to support each critique.
	b. Identify gaps in knowledge/research.
	c. Explain any development of traditions that have been established but not fully investigated.
	d. Present arguments for introducing any new perspective or theoretical framework(as a result of Unit 1 claims).
3. Announice how you will occupy the research gapv.	a. Announce the aim (s) of your study.
	b. Announce the relevant framework (s).
	c. Announce the key research design and processes.

9.2.3 Analysis of the Sample Thesis

In this section, we will take a look at the various content units and sub-units used in one thematic unit of our sample thesis.

1) Reporting Theoretical Perspectives

The sample of this section is the first part of the literature review chapter of the master's thesis, of which the focus is on the way of reporting theoretical perspectives of the research field.

1. Motivation is viewed as a "key factor in L2 learning" in second language acquisition (SLA) research (Ellis, 1994, p. 508; Skehan 1989). The study of the role of motivation in SLA has been a prominent research area in the second language field (DÖrnyei and Kormos, 2000). The most important and influential motivation theory specific to second language learning has been proposed by Robert Gardner, Wallace Lambert and associates (Skehan, 1989; DÖrnyei 2001), who "grounded motivation research in a social psychological framework" (DÖrnyei, 1994, p. 273). Gardner and Lambert (1972) drew a distinction between integrative motivation and instrumental motivation. Integrative motivation is identified with positive attitudes toward a target language group and a willingness to integrate into that target community. Instrumental motivation, on the other hand, refers to functional and practical reasons for	Centrality, importance and claims

learning a second language, such as getting a job or a promotion, or to pass a required examination.	
2. Gardner (1985) established socio-educational model to account for the role of various individual differences in the learning of a second language. This model proposes two basic attitudes—integrativeness and "attitudes toward the learning situation". Integrativeness refers to the desire to learn a second language to meet and communicate with members of the L2 community whereas "attitudes toward the learning situation" refers to learners' reaction to formal instruction (Gardner and MacIntyre, 1993). These two classes of variables contribute to learners' levels of L2 motivation which, in turn, influences language learning outcomes in both formal and informal learning situations (MacIntyre and Charos, 1996). Gardner's approach has influenced many studies in L2 motivation and has had direct empirical support in the field of second and foreign language education (Gardner, 1988). Yet in spite of this influence, results found in some studies were contradictory. For example, studies by Oller and his associates reported negative relationships between integrativeness measures and proficiency (Skehan, 1989). Gardner himself had admitted that no link necessarily existed between integrative attitudes and proficiency, and also acknowledged that the patterns of relationships among attitudinal and motivational variables and learning outcomes found in various studies were unstable (1985).	Claims Critique and evidence Critique
3. A noticeable "educational shift" occurred in motivation research during the 1990s, a period of feverish research activity in L2 learning motivation. In particular, the period was marked by a search for new learning motivation paradigms, as well as an expansion of the scope, in both theory and practice of L2 learning motivation. The most influential pioneering works were provided by Crookes and Schmidt (1991), DÖrnyei (1994), Oxford and Shearin (1994). Crookes and Schmidt (1991) criticized the dominance of Gardner's social psychological approach, offering instead a motivational framework made up of four components. These were interest, relevance, xpectancy and satisfaction/outcome. According to the authors, these variables provided an alternative to Gardner's integrative/instrumental dichotomy (DÖrnyei, 2001). DÖrnyei (1994) criticized Gardner's model because, in his view, its main emphasis relied on general motivational components grounded in a social milieu rather than in the foreign language classroom. He thus called for a more pragmatic and education-centered approach to language learning motivation. In this he followed an approach taken earlier by Crookes and Schmidt (1991), by examining motivation at micro, classroom, curriculum and extracurricular levels, then synthesizing them into a three-level framework — language level, learner level and learning situation level. Oxford and Shearin's (1994) study addressed a growing gap between L2 motivation theories and the emerging concepts in mainstream motivational psychology. They argued that the integrative/instrumental view of motivation was too narrow and offered alternative ways by which the notion of L2 motivation might be considered.	Critique and new perspective Critique and new perspective Critique and evidence

Yet, at the same time, they called for an expansion of the social psychological approach. A common thread running through the literature mentioned above was a view suggesting that Gardner's theory was so influential and dominant, that alternative concepts were not seriously considered (Crookes and Schmidt, 1991, p. 50l; DÖrnyei, 1994, p. 274).	Critique and new perspective
4. In response to criticism and calls for the adaptation of a wider vision of motivation (for example, Crookes and Schmidt, 1991, DÖrnyei 1994, Oxford and Shearin, 1994), Trembtay and Gardner (1995) extended Gardner's earlier construct of L2 motivation and proposed a new structural model. They incorporated three alternative motivational theories into the model. The first is the goal theory, for which Oxford and Shearin (1994) suggested that learners' personal goals in language learning situations should be set specifically in ways that were challenging but achievable, and accompanied by appropriate feedback about progress. The second is the attribution theory, intended to explain why subjective reasons to which learners attributed their past successes and failures considerably shaped their motivational disposition (DÖrnyei, 2003, p. 8). The third is the self-efficacy theory, in which self-efficacy refers to a learners' judgment of how well he can execute course of actions (Oxford and Shearin, 1994), or an individual's beliefs that he has the ability to reach a certain level of performances (Tremblay and Gardner, 1995). Their model was empirically tested and supported to reveal that motivation was a socially	New Perspective
and psychologically complex construct (Tremblay and Gardner, 1995; Gardner et al, 1997).	Evidence
5. The new approaches explored during the 1990s moved towards a wider direction in theorizing motivation, rather than a simple focus on the social psychological dimension (DÖrnyei, 1998). Gardner's (1985) approach offered a macro perspective in which "L2 motivation was examined in a broad sense, by focusing on the learners' over-all and generalized disposition towards learning the L2" (DÖrnyei, 2002). This macro perspective was however criticized as being "less adequate for providing a fine-tuned analysis of instructed Second Language Acquisition (SLA), which takes place primarily in language classrooms" (DÖrnyei, 2003, p. 11). But the 1990s movement did place greater emphasis on a more situated approach, and shifted from social attitudes to classroom reality, with more and more studies investigating how student motivation was reflected in concrete classroom situations (DÖrnyei, 1994, 2002). Recent research directions that have adopted this situated approach have been characterized by a micro perspective that included the study of task motivation and the study of willingness to communicate (DÖrnyei, 2003).	Claims

Paragraph 1 introduces this theme/topic unit with statements about the centrality and importance of motivation in Second Language Acquisition. And thenit introduces a key knowledge statement about the theoretical background underpinning the role of motivation in SLA (Second Lan-

guage Acquisition). The knowledge claims presented in sentences 4~6 define two key motivation constructs. Thus, three different aspects of the knowledge territory of motivation in SLA have been introduced: its importance, its theoretical significance and its construct components.

Paragraph 2 describes and explains the contribution of this early theoretical perspective before explaining that it has not gone unchallenged. This paragraph begins by presenting a number of knowledge claims and theoretical claims and research evidence in support of the theoretical model mentioned. Then the evidence presented is critiqued by telling that some studies have revealed contradictory findings. The author, then offers a resolution to these two positions. In doing so, the author is indirectly exposing a gap or an area of investigation that needs to be further investigated.

Paragraph 3 then presents a chronological outline of developments in theoretical claims and with arguments about second language learning motivation. Throughout the paragraph, each of the sentences is concerned with a critique of the Gardner and associates' perspectives because of the limited nature of their focus and therefore of their sole relevance to motivation in the second language learning classroom setting. Finally, the paragraph summarizes "the common thread running through the literature mentioned above" — the dominance of Gardner's theory (referred to in paragraph 2), that is, to the point where other perspectives on motivation were ignored. And this is new perspective opening the place for further investigation and research.

Paragraph 4 presents the response to these claims, following on from the critique and call for "a wider vision of motivation". This paragraph first introduces the new theoretical model proposed by Tremblay and Gardner in 1995, then describes the alternative motivation theories that were incorporated into the new model, finally, explains how research evidence showed that motivation was a socially and psychologically complex construct, thereby supporting the arguments expressed in paragraph 3 about the inadequacy of Gardner's original perspective.

Paragraph 5 sums up the developments presented in the first four paragraphs, starting with summary statements of the overall focus and significance of developments in the 1990s. The paragraph ends with a statement about the influence of these developments on recent research — a focus on empirically testing micro perspectives like task motivation and a willingness to communicate. Thus, the final sentence provides a link to the next unit of the literature review on task motivation.

2) Conclusion of Literature Review

The conclusion of the literature review will usually start with a summary of the key claims that have been presented in this part. In doing so, the author will usually draw some conclusions about the claims and involve an evaluation or the importance and significance of the claims. Having done this, the author will identify gaps or shortcomings in this literature and explain why one or more of the gaps should be filled. Finally, the conclusion will introduce the reader to an announcement of the aim(s) and/or research question(s) of the study; it will draw up an outline of the key theoretical perspectives, the methodology, design, processes.

In the following sample thesis, you can see the conclusion part of the literature review and observe the way in which it realizes the function of a concluding part.

1. This chapter has reviewed literature concerned with three areas of critical importance in this present research. Firstly, the literature that addresses motivation, with a particular focus on the development of motivational research — the shift from a macro social psychological approach to a micro situated approach to motivation —was described. Two research paradigms, as being representative of this situated approach to motivation, were identified as task motivation and willingness to communicate. A consideration of task motivation research then followed. It also presented the WTC construct and examined the WTC construct from differing perspectives. Empirical studies that explored the potential antecedents and consequences of WTC in L2 were reviewed. Finally, it foreshadows the operationalization of the WTC construct as an appropriate variable for study in a second language classroom. This contention is based on observations made in the earlier literature concerned with WTC.	Summary of main topics presented in the review
2. Yet it should be pointed out that, until now, very little empirical research concerning WTC in L2 appears to have been done by a combination of quantitative and qualitative methods. Because of the predominant use of questionnaires, WTC research to date has tended to focus on reported WTC rather than actual classroom behavior. A number of researchers have actually called for verification of self-report WTC data by behavioral studies of the L2 classroom (MacIntyre and Charos, 1996). Moreover, variations in WTC over time that would on the face of it, inject a dynamic aspect into WTC research, appear to have been largely ignored in previous studies. Moreover, further research concerned with how WTC changes over time appears to be needed.	Various research gaps
3. This study is an attempt to fill these gaps by exploring learners' WTC behavior in a second language classroom within a task-based framework. Four key research questions are thus raised below to investigate whether an individual learner's WTC behavior changes according to three different situational contexts in a second language classroom over a period of a second language course as well as exploring factors that might affect WTC behavior from learners' perspective. Does learners' self-report of WTC correspond to their behavior in class in three interactional contexts: whole class, small groups and pair work?	Research questions and methodology
Does learners' WTC behavior in class differ according to three different contexts: whole class, small groups and pair work? Does learners' WTC behavior in class change over time in the case of this study in a one-month course? What are learners' perceptions of most important factors contributing to their WTC in three classroom contexts?	

Paragraph 1 is a summary of the main themes/topics presented in the body of the review.

Paragraph 2 summarizes the various gaps that have been identified in the body of the review. It points out the various shortcomings in the methodological approaches.

Paragraph 3 explains that the research project being reported in the thesis investigated the gaps identified in paragraph 3 and the methodological framework. Finally, announces the aims and 4 research questions that guided the study, together with the context and duration of the investigation.

3) Some Key Linguistic Features of a Literature Review

The literature review provides the reader with the background to fully understand the context of your study and why it was worth doing (Galvan, 2009). In doing this, the "argument" that is developed throughout the literature review reports on and critiques a range of published literature. The skills that are required to do this effectively are several, so this section will outline some of the major ones.

Reporting the Published Literature

There are two main reasons for reporting what others have said (Hart, 1998).

The first reeson is to explain what has been reported in the literature and what has not been reported (including gaps in the published literature). The second reeson is to evaluate the work of others in order to negotiate your position. Here, we will focus our attention on some of the knowledge and skills that are required for explaining what has been reported in the literature. Two of the main types of reporting(Hart, 2005) are presented below with the examples.

(1) Central reporting — author responsible for claim is the subject of the sentence.

e.g. McCrosksy (1992, p. 21) concluded that the assumptions were tenable…

(2) Non-central reporting — names of author responsible for claim is placed in brackets at the end of a sentence.

e.g. Yet the WTC scale appeared to offer the best instrument, in measuring the WTC construct (McCrosksy and Richmond, 1987).

Choice of Reporting Verb

Authors need to take care when choosing their reporting verbs. Because of the similarity in meaning of some verbs, you can easily misrepresent another author if the reporting verb is not accurate or fails to convey the exact aspects of meaning (Swales, 2004). For example, because there is only a slight difference in meaning between the verbs "state" and "claim", it is important that the appropriate and precise verb be chosen to convey the source. Comparing the difference amorg verbs such as "noted", "stated", "argued", "contended", "claimed" and "established", it can be seen that each of these verbs conveys a greater strength of claim. In the following sample thesis, varying strength of verbs that have been chosen to report the various claims have been displayed.

e.g. Gardner(1985) ***established*** *socio-educational model to account for the role of various individual differences in the learning of a second language. This model proposes two basic attitudes*

— integrativeness and "attitudes toward the learning situation"... These two classes of variables **contribute** to learners' levels of L2 motivation which... Gardner's approach has **influenced** many studies in L2 motivation... Yet in spite of this influence, results **found** in some studies were contradictory. For example, studies by Oiler and his associates **reported** negative relationships between integrativeness measures and proficiency... Gardner himself **had admitted** that no link necessarily existed between integrative attitudes and proficiency, and also **acknowledged** that the patterns of relationships of attitudinal and motivational variables and learning outcomes found in various studies were unstable (1985).

Tense of Reporting Verbs

Even within a single paragraph the choice of tenses for reporting claims or propositions can vary a great deal. Reasons for using particular tenses are presented below (Seliger & Shohamy, 1989).

(1) Present simple is used to convey the current state of knowledge, to make a generalization and to present earlier findings as accepted facts.

(2) Past simple is used to refer to a claim or finding that has been made.

(3) Present perfect is used to refer to the currently accepted state of affairs.

Now you can see the use of different tenses in the following sample thesis paragraph and the key verbs has been highlighted for easier identification.

e. g. These two classes of variables **contribute** to learners' levels of L2 motivation which, in turn, influences language learning outcomes in both formal and informal learning situations (MacIntyre and Charos, 1996). Gardner's approach has **influenced** many studies in L2 motivation and has had direct empirical support in the field of second and foreign language education (Gardner, 1988). Yet in spite of this influence, results **found** in some studies were contradictory.

9.3 Methodology

This section will focus on the functions of the methodology chapter. It is about the content that should be included and how to most effectively organize the content. This is often a relatively straight forward chapter to write because the issues and processes that need to be presented will have been considered before the data were collected and notes may well have been made before and during the data collection process. It is important to have a clear understanding of the aims and functions of the chapter.

9.3.1 The Function of a Thesis Methodology Chapter

The key aims of this chapter will be to describe and justify the methodological approach, the research design, the data collection and analytical processes you followed. The specific functions of the chapter will therefore include the following aspects (Bitchener, 2018).

The first is A description and justification of the methodological approach.

The second is A description and justification of the research design.

The third is A description and justification of the specific methods employed for data collection.

The fourth is A discussion of ways in which the validity and reliability of the data were achieved.

The fifth is A description and justification of the data collection procedures.

The sixth is A description and justification of the data analysis procedures.

Although there is a built-in logic to the order in which the functions might be achieved, a logical argument can be achieved by describing and justifying the data collection processes before or after describing and justifying the design and methods employed in the study.

9.3.2 The Content and Structure of a Thesis Methodology Chapter

The table below (which has been introduced in Chapter 7) shows the possibility of a logical argument in methodology chapter. The thing to note is that the lists of sub-units presented here are quite comprehensive but not exhaustive. You may consider other sub-units should be added in order to ensure a full description and justification of your methodology. As we have done in the previous chapters, we will now consider the ways in which the methodology chapter of one sample thesis was presented.

Main units	Sub-units
1. Present the procedures for measuring the variables of your research.	a. Describe and justify the methodological approach of the study from a philosophical perspective.
	b. Define, describe and justify the methods of measuring the variables of your study.
2. Explain the data collection procedures.	a. Describe the sample(e.g.location, size, characteristics, context, ethical issues).
	b. Describe the instruments used for data collection; describe the validity and reliability or truthfulness measures.
	c. Describe the steps of the data collection procedures.
	d. Justify a~c, highlighting advantages and disadvantages, in light of research aim (s) and research questions/hypotheses.
3. Explain the data analysis procedures.	a. Describe, illustrate and justify the data analysis procedures.

9.3.3 Sample Analysis of a Thesis Methodology Chapter

The sample was chosen from a methodology chapter of a PhD dissertation (Ku, 2016). In this section, the focus of the analysis will be on how the content units are realized in the chapter.

1) Introduction of the Chapter

1. In the U.S., nearly two-thirds of first-time community college students were required to take at least one developmental course in mathematics (Bahr, 2013). Despite the assistance and training they received in developmental courses, approximately 75% of those students did not successfully complete a mathematics course at the college level (Bahr, 2013; Fain, 2012). Consequently, about	Reason of choosing the methodology for the study

50% of first-time community college students did not obtain a degree (Bahr, 2012). Research has shown that the higher the college completion rate is the better the economy of a country is (Davidovitch, Byalsky, Soen, & Sinuani-Stern, 2013). If the graduation rates continue to decline, the U.S. may lose its global competitiveness.

2. One factor that led to low completion rates in developmental mathematics courses was the ineffectiveness of instructional strategies (Yuksel, 2010). It has been shown that — to be continued using a TLM strategy on students in the twenty-first century did not improve their motivation toward learning or academic achievement (Nafees, Farooq, Shaheen, & Akhtar, 2012). On the other hand, positive correlations between the incorporation of TBL strategies and student motivation and academic performance were documented in multiple disciplinary studies (Hsiung, 2012; Wong & Abbruzzese, 2011). Although TBL is becoming a favorable teaching strategy, the face-to-face lecture style remains the most common instructional methods at the college level (Carlson, 2013). In order to increase college completion rates for all students, improving student-learning experiences in developmental mathematics courses has becoming a growing national commitment (Cullinane & Treisman, 2010; Goldstein, Burke, Getz, Kennedy, 2011). Therefore, there was a need to measure the differences in individual student motivation and achievement in developmental mathematics courses as a result of incorporating TLM strategy as opposed to TBL strategy.	
3. The purpose of this quantitative, ex post facto study was to examine the differences in individual student motivation and achievement in developmental mathematics courses as a result of incorporating TBL strategy as opposed to TLM strategy. The study site was at a community college in San Antonio, Texas. According to a power analysis via G*Power (Faul et al., 2009), the study required at least 42 students, who enrolled in a three-hour credit developmental mathematics course in the community college. However, a total of 44 students, in which 21 students in the TLM group and 23 students in the TBL group, participated in this study. In order to recruit participants, the TSI (CORD, 2010) was given to the professors in the participating institution. After identifying professors' teaching style to be either TLM or TBL, they distributed research materials along with a link to an online survey engine called SurveyMonkey® to students in their classes. The sample comprised of 21 students, who experienced a traditional face-to-face lecture style without the incorporation of social learning strategy, and 23 students, who received instruction that utilized a specific TBL strategy, called the SLO. In order to measure student motivation, participants completed the pre and post CIS (Keller, 2010), which assessed learners' motivation reaction to specific instructional environment. Each participant provided demographic information, as a part of the CIS, in order for information on sex, ethnicity, and age to be	Appropriateness of choosing the methodology

collected. Demographic information of students, including gender, ethnicity, and age was used as descriptive data. A comparison of student achievement was based on the differences of the pre and post ASQ (College Board, 2012). A one-way MANOVA was used to measure the differences of incorporating TBL strategy on individual student motivation and achievement in college developmental mathematics courses.	
4. Chapter 3 will begin with a description of the research methods and designs and information about the population and the sample. Materials and instruments will be described, and the operational definition of variables will be provided. Data collection, processing, and analysis will be discussed in detail. Assumptions, limitations, delimitation, and ethical assurances will be elaborated. This chapter will be concluded with a summary.	Outline of the Methodological approach
5. Corresponding to the problem and purpose statements, the following research questions guided the study. Q1. To what extent, if any, is there a difference in student motivation, as measured by the post-pre CIS, between the learning environment of TLM and TBL, among students in developmental mathematics courses at one community college in San Antonio, Texas? Q2. To what extent, if any, is there a difference in student achievement, as measured by the post-pre ASQ, between the learning environment of TLM and TBL, among students in developmental mathematics courses at one community college in San Antonio, Texas?	Research questions

Paragraph 1~2 explains why the methodological approach and research design have been chosen, namely, that they are the best suited to the investigation of the research.

Paragraph 3 reveals that the quantitative, ex post facto method was chosen as the most appropriate for the research purpose.

Paragraph 4 illustrates the specific process of data collection and an overview of how it will be analyzed.

Paragraph 5 restates the research questions which are used as a guidance for the methodelogy chapter.

2) Research Methods and Design

6. An ex post facto approach was appropriate for this quantitative study because a true experiment for this study was not possible due to the reality that not all instructors are required to incorporate TBL in their teaching (Campbell & Stanley, 1996; Cook & Campbell, 1979). In addition, a true experiment requires randomized assignment of subjects, which is impossible at a college setting because professors cannot use two different instructional styles on students at the same time in the same class (Shadish, Cook, & Campbell, 2002). An ex post facto research	Research method with justification

was used, rather than simple correlation research, because this quantitative study focused on measuring the differences in individual student motivation and achievement in developmental mathematics courses as a result of incorporating TBL as a treatment versus TLM. Therefore, the use of intervention, treatments, and post assessments were needed in order to measure and compare the two learning environments (M. Gall, J. Gall, & Borg, 2007). A descriptive approach was not considered because this study aimed to validate hypotheses (B. Cook & L. Cook, 2008; Dobrovolny & Fuentes, 2008). Considering the needs to answer all the research questions, a quantitative, ex post facto design fitted the best for this study.	
7. Several stages were needed in order to recruit participants and collect data. First, an approval of Institutional Review Board (IRB) was needed from both Northcentral University and the participating institution. Second, in order to recruit professors, who dominantly use either TLM or TBL strategies, email invitations for participation were sent to 12 professors, who taught developmental mathematics courses at the participating institution. If a professor indicated interest in participation, then he or she signed an informed consent form before the 12-question TSI (CORD, 2010) was completed. Scores of each survey items were totaled, and a teaching style was determined as a guide by the Center for Occupational Research and Development (CORD, 2010). Based on the TSI scores, professors were classified by teaching style to be either TLM or TBL. Post-pre assessments were used to measure any differences in student motivation and achievement as a result of participating in a	Description of procedure with justification
specific teaching style. In order to measure changes in student motivation, the professors distributed materials to all participating students to take the 16-question CIS (Keller, 2010), which took an average of 10 to 15 minutes to complete, before and after the treatment. The purpose of the CIS was to assess the level of learners' motivation corresponding to a specific instructional environment (Razzouk, 2011). Each participant also provided demographic information, as a part of the CIS, in order for information on sex, ethnicity, and age to be collected, which was used as descriptive data. Similarly, changes in student achievement because of a teaching style was measured by the 20-question ASQ sample questions (College Board, 2012). After all data were collected, SPSS version 23 was used to conduct a MANOVA in order to answer each of the research questions and to test the hypotheses (IBM Corp, 2013).	
Population 8. The population described in this study was community college students in the U.S., who were required to take at least one developmental mathematics course. Nearly two million students in the U.S. were enrolled in remedial classes annually (Jones et al., 2012). Statistics have shown that ethnicities and college readiness in mathematics are related; for example, the percentages of student who were required	

to take a developmental mathematics course corresponding to their ethnicities were as the following: 64% African-American, 49% Hispanic and Latino, 35% Native American, and 21% White (CSU Online Database, 2010). Nationally, community college enrollment by ethnicity was categorized as the following: 68% White and non-Hispanic; 27% Black and non-Hispanic; 1% Hispanic; 1% Asian and Pacific Islander; and 3% others (AACC, 2015). Nearly 61% of students enrolled were female, and about 39% were male (AACC, 2015). In Texas, about 49% of community college students were White and non-Hispanic, 30% were Hispanic, 12% were Asian and Pacific Islander, 4% were Asian, and 5% were others (AACC, 2015). The percentage of female student enrollment (58%) versus male student enrollment (42%) was about the same as the national (AACC, 2015). Those college students were required to take at least one developmental courses in mathematics (Bahr, 2013; Bailey et al., 2010). Although the described population in this study was community college students who enrolled in mathematics developmental courses, time and financial limitations made random sampling impossible for this study. Instead, a purposive sampling was used to represent the sample. The study site was at the community college in San Antonio, Texas. The enrollment consisted of 55% female and 45% male; enrollment by ethnicity was categorized as the following: 57% Hispanic, 28% White, 6% Black, 3% Asian, and 6% others (NVC, 2015). The number of students enrolled at the study site was about 16674, and the number of students enrolled in a developmental mathematics course was about 1500 per semester (NVC, 2014b).	Location, size, context, characteristics
Sample 9. Based on an a priori power analysis for a MANOVA via G*Power (Faul et al., 2009), version 3.1.9.2 with = 0.05, power = 0.80 (Cohen, 1989), two groups, two response variables, and effect size of 0.25, this study comprised of 44 students altogether, who enrolled in a three-hour credit developmental mathematics course in the community college. It has been reported, using a MANOVA with an indication of 44.5% of overall variation, that the learning environment has statistically significant effects on student achievement and motivation (Strayer, 2012). In addition, research included the result from the ANOVA, where the level of motivation demonstrated 76% of overall variation, to show a significant difference in student achievement with respect to student motivation (Vansteenkiste, Sierens, Soenens, Luyckx, & Lens, 2009). However, a conservative effect size was used to calculate the required sample size. A total of 44 students, in which 21 students in the TLM group and 23 students in the TBL group, participated in this study. Participant recruitment started with identifying professors' instructional style. Email invitations were sent to 12 mathematics professors, who taught developmental courses in Fall 2015. The enrollment for each developmental class was 25 students, and the study required a minimum of 42 students all together (Faul et al., 2009). It was estimated	Location, size, context, characteristics

that five classes were needed because statistics showed that the response rate for online surveys was approximately 40% (Archer, 2008; Perkins, 2011). After consents were obtained from professors, their teaching style was determined by completing the instrument called the TSI (CORD, 2010). Students of the participating professors then handed out materials along with an online link to their students as an invitation to participate in this study. Students, who wanted to participate, signed an informed consent form prior to their participation. Students also filled out their email addresses, in order to be contacted and receive reminders electronically. All professors and students, who turned in their informed consent forms, were considered for participation. In order to encourage participation, the following incentives were offered to professors and students. Professors, who agreed and implemented the SLO activities once a week for four consecutive weeks, received a $50 Amazon.com e-gift card. Participating students, who successfully completed the pre and post CIS and ASQ, were eligible to enter the drawing pool for a chance to win a $20 Amazon.com e-gift card.

Materials/Instruments

10. Three instruments were used in this study in order to answer the research questions. Written permissions to use each instrument were obtained prior to recruiting participants and gathering data. The first instrument was the TSI which determined the teaching styles of mathematics teachers. The TSI had 12 questions with four statements in each question describing how a person teaches. Participants ranked the four statements in each question with scales from one (1) to four (4), with a "4" being the most descriptive statement that matched his or her response and the next most descriptive statement should receive a "3," then a "2," and finally a "1" being the least descriptive statement. Professors completed the 12-question TSI (CORD, 2010), and each survey item was summed up as a guide by the CORD in order to determine teaching style. Based on the TSI scores, professors were classified by teaching style to be either TLM or TBL. The second instrument was the 16-question CIS, which measured a student's reactions corresponding to classroom instruction (Keller, 2010). The CIS measured student motivation in four subscales: attention (4 items), which measured learners' interests in learning the course materials; relevance (4 items), which measured learners' level of connection between course materials and personal goals; confidence (4 items), which measured learners' level of self-assurances, and satisfaction (4 items), which measured learners' level of self-fulfillment of learning expectations (Keller, 1987). Each subscale in the CIS included four questions using a 5-point graded Likert scale, ranging from "not true" (1) to "very true" (5), were provided for each survey question (Karoulis, 2011). The response scale was ranged from one (1) to five (5) for each of the 16 statements. The last instrument was the ASQ (College Board, 2012), which contained 20 multiple-choice mathematics questions corresponding to the curriculum

(margin note: Instruments with justification)

standards guided by the SACS and the THECB. The College Board and Educational Testing Service established the ACCUPLACER testing program in 1985, and its main function was to determine if high school graduates were ready to take core courses at the college level (Elliot et al., 2012). The results and analyses from each of the three instruments were intended to be used to answer the research questions and validate the hypotheses.

Having analyzed the research method and design section of the methodology chapter, we can make a number of overall observations about the content and structure.

(1) The author begins with a consideration of the methodology. The basis upon which the methodological approach would be most suitable was explained, citing reasons for adopting an ex post facto approach which is a practice of quantitative methods. In doing so, reasons for why an ex post facto research was used, rather than simple correlation research was pointed out. Then, several stages for recruiting participants and collecting data were introduced with justifications of supporting reasons.

(2) Another noteworthy feature of this section of the chapter is the frequent use of supporting literature to support the claims and options presented in the definitions, descriptions and justifications. The author's focus was almost exclusively on defining, describing and justifying the methodology and methods chosen for the study.

(3) Details of the characteristics of the participants that the author believes the reader should know are presented in "participation" and "sample" part, including background, gender ratio, age, learning background and learning context. There are two details that one might also consider, including providing a heading that includes the word "context" as well as "participants" or "sample" and providing source justification for including the particular sample in the study. Concerning the latter, the reader might also find it useful to know why the particular proficiency level and context were chosen.

(4) In the instrument section, the author introduces three methods employed in the data collection. Each of these methods was explained to give a clear picture of how the research data to be collected. If we consider the whole of this section as one unit, sometimes, an author will also find it necessary to discuss the disadvantages of using a particular method, so this will typically be presented before or after the advantages (Rudestam & Newton, 2001). In the sample thesis, the author has explained how to implement particular method to solve each aspect of the research questions.

(5) Having described the methodological options available and having described and justified the methodological approach and the specific methods chosen for her study, the author has set the stage for detailing the specific characteristics of the data processing and analysis.

3) *Data Processing and Analysis*

1. A one-way MANOVA, conducted by SPSS, was used to generate analyses in order to determine the differences in student motivation and achievement between the two learning groups, TLM versus TBL, after a four-week treatment period. A one-way MANOVA was chosen for the analytical method because there were two related dependent variables, and the test provided details for the differences in student motivation. One assumption of MANOVA was that there was no multicollinearity, meaning that the dependent variables were moderate correlated (Meyers, Gamst, & Guarino, 2006). Having a high or low multicollinearity could decrease liability (Grewal, Cote, & Baumgartner, 2004). One way to check multicollinearity was by using SPSS to perform a Multiple Linear Regression (MLR). In order to generate a Variance Inflation Factor (VIF) value, the dependent variables, motivation and achievement, were ran as the independent variables of the MLR. It was recommended that the VIF value was between 1 and 10 (Lin, 2008). Another assumption of MANOVA was the homogeneity of variances; therefore, the signification level reported by a Levene's test needed to be greater than 0.05 (Betz, 1987). According to a power analysis via G*Power (Faul et al., 2009), the study required a minimum of 42 students. When the number of participants reached the requirement of the power analysis, it was assumed that the samples were large enough so that the multivariate normality assumption holds. However, a test for skewness and kurtosis was conducted to determine normality. The other assumption was that the observations were independent, meaning that students were in the group of either TLM or TBL, so that no participant participated in both groups. A multivariate mode under the general linear model was the method to analyze the data.	Outline and justification of data analysis & processing method
2. For the first null hypothesis (H10: There is no significant difference in student motivation, as measured by the post-pre CIS, between a learning environment of TLM and TBL, among students in developmental mathematics courses), the statistical significance in motivation score between students in TLM and TBL was examined. To determine statistically significant differences, a one-way MANOVA was conducted in order to obtain a mu ltivariate F value. The significance of the main effect of student motivation was used to answer research question 1.	Justification according to research question
3. For the second null hypothesis (H20: There is no significant difference in student achievement, as measured by the post-pre CIS, between a learning environment of TLM and TBL, among students in developmental mathematics courses), the statistical significance in achievement score between students in TLM and TBL was examined. To determine statistically significant differences, a one-way MANOVA was conducted in order to obtain a multivariate F value. The significance of the main effect of student achievement was used to answer research question 2.	

In writing this section of a thesis, first decision needs to be made on the extent to which you are going to provide specific detail and illustrations from the thesis of analytical processes or whether this level of detail is going to be more helpful for the reader. Once the decision has been made, the focus should be on the outline of the key analytical and processing measures with the justification of the practice. And then the further justification can be provided according to the effectiveness of the data analysis method to solve/answer research questions.

4) Ethical Assurances

> This research involved human subjects. IRB approvals from the study site and Northcentral University were granted prior to any data collection. A certificate of Collaborative Institutional Training Initiative (CITI) was obtained as required by Northcentral University. Participants were informed that their participation in the study was voluntary, and for students, refusal of participation would not affect their grades in the course. Similarly, student participants did not receive extra credits toward the course for completing the research. There were no more than minimum risks in this study.
>
> Participating professors distributed study materials to their students, and if a student agreed to participate in this study, a signed consent form, which described the purpose, duration, and procedure of the study, was needed prior to completing the surveys. Participants had the opportunities to ask any questions regarding the procedures of this study and had the right to stop participating at any time. Participants were informed that the highest ethical standards are upheld in order to protect the identities of the participants. For example, the surveys will be kept in an encrypted device and participants' real names will remain anonymous in the research paper. An alphanumeric coding system was used in order to maintain anonymity and confidentiality. All data will be stored in primary researcher's computer with a secured file encryption in case of the equipment being lost or stolen. After the research is finished, data collected will be kept in the encrypted device for seven years, and the device will be formatted thereafter. It was anticipated that no psychological harm, physical harm, legal harm, social harm, or economic harm would occur in this entire process of data collection. Therefore, there were no more than minimum risks of participating in the study. Participants were informed that the responses in the surveys are only used for research purposes. There were no benefits to the individuals directly. The guidelines of ethical assurances instructed in Northcentral University were observed for this study.

The focus of any section on ethical issues is on identifying the issues and explaining how they were addressed(Dörnyei, 2007). As you read the text in the box above, you will see that this is exactly what the author has done. Each of the sentences describes how the privacy and confidentiality of the participants were addressed. IRB should be officially approved. Essentially, the text outlines the key statements presented in the Consent Form presented in the appendices. Depending on the specific requirements of a university or a journal, authors may add to or modify the approach taken here. And assurance of the security of information collected from the data collection should be described. Furthermore, authors need to guarantee to protect participants' privacy and permit that the data collected are for research purpose only.

5) Summary

1. Research has shown that in the U.S., approximately two-thirds of first-time community college students were required to take at least one developmental course in mathematics (Bahr, 2013; Bailey et al., 2010). Three-fourths of those students did not complete a college level course (Bahr, 2013; Fain, 2012).

2. The purpose of this quantitative, ex post facto study was to measure the differences in individual student motivation and achievement in developmental mathematics courses, as a result of incorporating TBL as a treatment versus TLM. The quantitative, ex post facto design was chosen for this study because the research questions and hypotheses in this study were designed and aimed to be validated by using the statistical methods (B. Cook & L. Cook, 2008; Dobrovolny & Fuentes, 2008). In addition, time and financial limitation made it unpractical to conduct individual interviews for all college students in America (Krathwohl, 1998; Mason, 1996). An ex post facto approach was appropriate for this quantitative study because a true experiment for this study was not possible due to the reality that not all instructors are required to incorporate TBL in their teaching (Campbell & Stanley 1996, Cook & Campbell, 1979). Combining all the reasons, a quantitative, ex post facto approach served the best for the needs of this study, than a qualitative or mixed method.

3. The study site was at a community college in San Antonio, Texas. AG*Power indicated that the study required at least 42 students, who enrolled in a three-hour credit developmental mathematics course in the community college (Faul, 2010). Based on the results of the TSI, two groups of participants, TLM and TBL, were identified. A total of 44 students, in which 21 students in the TLM group and 23 students in the TBL group, participated in this study. A specific TBL strategy, called the SLO developed by the professors and researchers at the participating institution, under the guideline of the SACS and the THECB, was used as the treatment by the participating professors, who identified themselves as TBL instructors, once a week for four consecutive weeks for standardization.

4. Three instruments were used in this study. First, the 12-question TSI developed by CORD was used (CORD, 2010) to categorize professors' teaching styles to be either TLM or TBL. Second, the 16-question CIS (Keller, 2010), which measured student motivation, was completed by all participating students before and after the four-week treatment period. Third, the 20-question ASQ (College Board, 2012) was used to measure each participating student's mathematics achievement before and after the treatment. Written permission to use each instrument along with IRB approvals was obtained prior to data collection.

5. The independent variable, which included two types of learning environment, TLM and TBL, was the grouping variable for this study. The dependent variables, academic achievement and motivation in learning, were the outcomes after the treatment. SPSS was used to conduct a one-way MANOVA in order to answer each of the research questions and to test the hypotheses (IBM Corp, 2013).

The final section of the chapter summarizes the main content areas of the chapter. In some respects, it is a little bit like a shopping list but, if clear cohesive links are made between sentences, it will read more effectively as a summary of the overall argument underpinning the methodological approach of the study. The text in the Box above can be a very good example. Paragraph 1 states the need or the gap for the research of this study; paragraph 2 justifies the design of the method for the study; paragraph 3 summarizes the condition and context of participants; paragraph 4 briefs the instruments, while paragraph 5 focuses on the data processing and analysis. This summary is a thorough conclusion of all the aspects mentioned in this chapter and is a miniature of the chapter by mentioning all the key points.

6) The Difference Between "Methodology" and "Method"

"Methodology" refers to the theoretical approach or framework that your study was situated in (Mackey & Gass, 2005). As such, it will explain the extent to which you employed a quantitative, qualitative and/or multi-method approach. You will need to explain why you chose the approach that was used in your study. This will involve some reference back to the research questions/hypotheses and issues you investigated. Illustration of methodology needs to refer to the literature available on research methodology and on research already published in the area of investigation so that argument can be presented for the approach adopted for the study.

"Method" refers to the specific methods you employed in your data collection (Mackey & Gass, 2005). Thus, you will need to describe the instruments and materials you used and explain why they were appropriate for the research questions/hypotheses you were investigating. The "methodology" will have informed the choice of "methods"(Bruce, 2008). In explaining why you chose particular methods, you will need to explain why they were chosen rather than other methods. Your justification will need to refer to the particular advantages that one method has over another. Inevitably, there will be some issues that you may not have been able to address, so these need to be acknowledged as limitations. Authors often refer to these in this chapter when talking about the scope or parameters of their study and refer to them again in the concluding chapter.

9.4 Results

This section focuses on the presentation of the results/findings of your study. This section begins with an outline of the functions of a results chapter before moving on to consider the content that needs to be presented and how it might be most effectively organized. This will be followed up with an analysis of sections of the sample thesis.

9.4.1 The Functions of a Thesis Results Chapter

The key purpose of this chapter is to present the findings from your investigation which enables the reader to understand with ease how they address your research questions/hypotheses. In doing so, you will need, at times, to refer back to material presented in your methodology and point the reader forward to what will be considered in the discussion of a results chapter. As you present each finding, you will also need to think about whether or not an explanation should be given about what the finding means. Evidence (e.g. statistics, examples, tables or figures) from your data and analysis will feature frequently as you support your findings. But, you will not need to comment further on the findings in this chapter. Various functions are summarized below (Bitchener, 2018).

(1) A presentation of the results/findings of your study that are relevant to your research questions/hypotheses.

(2) An explanation of what the findings mean (without interpretation).

(3) A presentation of evidence in support of your findings.

(4) References back to details of methodology and background/context.

(5) References forward to discussion of results issues.

9.4.2 The Content and Structure of a Thesis Resulta Chapter

The structure of the results chapter is mostly organized around the research questions/hypotheses. Having decided on the structure, authors will need to decide on the order in which the specific findings will be presented. As you set about introducing each new finding, you will then need to consider what further information should be given to support that finding. As can be seen in the table below (which has been introduced in Chapter 7), the content units can give the reader a full and clear understanding of each result. As has been done in other chapters, the presentation of a results chapter of the sample thesis will be presented.

Main units	Sub–units
1. Present brieflg any meta-textual information	a. Present any background information, methodological detail, references forward to the discussion chapter and links between sections that contextualize the results to be presented.
	b. Define, describe and justify the methods of measuring the variables of your study.
2. Present the results	a. Restate the research question/hypothesis.
	b. Present briefly any important procedures for generating the results that the reader should be reminded of.
	c. Present each result.
	d. Provide evidence for each result (e. g. statistics, examples, tables, figures).
	e. Explain what each result means.

9.4.3 Sample Analysis of the Thesis Results Chapter

The sample was also chosen from the results chapter of the same PhD dissertation (Ku, 2016) used in section 9.3. In this section, the focus of the analysis will be on how the content units are realized in the chapter.

1) Introduction of Results Chapter

The author begins her results chapter with an introduction (provided in Box below) to let the reader know how the results will be presented. The data collected during the research will be presented in a way that can answer the research questions of the study. Then the results will be presented in two main sections: each provides proofs for the hypotheses of the research questions.

1. The purpose of this quantitative, ex post facto study was to examine the differences in individual student motivation and achievement in developmental mathematics courses as a result of incorporating TBL strategy as opposed to TLM strategy. The sample consisted of 44 students, who were enrolled in a developmental mathematics course in Fall 2015, at a community college in San Antonio, Texas. In order to recruit student participants, the professors, who taught the developmental mathematics courses, received an invitation by email to complete the TSI (CORD, 2010). After identifying the professors' teaching style to be either TLM or TBL, the professors distributed the research materials with a web link to the study to their students. Students in each group, either TLM or TBL, completed the pre assessments, CIS (Keller, 2010) and ASQ (College Board, 2012), at the beginning of the semester, and they responded to the post assessments four weeks afterward. The instruments given to both groups were identical. However, students in the TBL group received instruction that utilized a specific TBL strategy, called the SLO. The independent variable in this study was the learning environment, either TBL or TLM, and it was determined based on the results of the TSI. The dependent variables were student motivation, measured by the post-pre CIS, and student achievement, as measured by the post-pre ASQ.	Background information Methodological details Justification of the measures of variables
2. Chapter 4 will start with introduction and results, followed by evaluation of the findings, and conclude with the summary. Demographic and descriptive statistics will be presented in the result section. Discussion will continue with the statistical analyses related to each research question. The evaluation of the findings related to both research questions and the literature review will be discussed. The summary will be provided at the end of Chapter 4.	Outline of this chapter

The overall structure of this chapter is clear and logical according to the content units mentioned in section 9.4.2. The point to note is the importance of signaling the approach to the reader in the introduction to the chapter.

2) Preliminary results presentation

3. A total of 12 professors, who taught the developmental mathematics courses in Fall 2015, were invited to take the TSI (CORD, 2010). Four professors, in which 50% were male and 50% were female, agreed and participated in the study. The age of the professors ranged from 46 to 62 years old ($M = 53$, $SD = 7.16$), and their ethnicities included Asian (25%), African American (25%), Hispanic (25%), and Caucasian (25%). The results of the TSI suggested that one male and one female professor were classified as TBL, and their ethnicities were African American and Caucasian; the other professors were categorized as TLM, and their ethnicities were Asian and Hispanic.	Demographic features of participants

4. A total of 120 students, who were enrolled in the developmental mathematics courses in Fall 2015, were invited to take the post-pre CIS (Keller, 2010) and the post-pre ASQ (College Board, 2012). Forty-five students in the TBL group completed the pre assessments, while 42 entries were collected from the TLM group. However, only 23 students in the TBL group and 21 students from the TLM group completed the post assessments. Nevertheless, the required sample size for each group was met, according to a power analysis via G*Power (Faul et al., 2009), which required at least 21 students in each group. Entries from participants, who did not complete the post assessments, were excluded. In the demographic survey, age was categorized into four subgroups, and they were 18 to 25, 26 to 35, 36 to 46, and above 46. In the TBL group, the percentage of each age subcategory was 56.5%, 26.1%, 13%, and 4.3%, respectively; while in the TLM group, all participants were either between 18 and 25 years old (95.2%) or between 26 and 35 years old (4.8%). Twenty-six percent of students were male and 74% were female in the TBL group, while 19% of students were male and 81% were female in the TLM group. Ethnicity was categorized into seven subgroups, and they were Asian, Black not Hispanic, Hispanic, Middle Eastern, multicultural, White not Hispanic, and other. In the TBL group, 4.3% were Black not Hispanic, 65.2% were Hispanic, and 30.4% were White not Hispanic; while in the TLM group, the percentages were 9.5%, 76.2%, and 14.3%, respectively.	Demographic features of participants
5. Students in both TBL and TLM groups were given the same pre and post assessments. The CIS had a maximum score of 80 and a minimum score of 16, and the ASQ had a maximum score of 100 and a minimum score of zero. In the TBL group, the pre CIS scores ranged from 50 to 80 (M = 70.22, SD = 8.18), and the post CIS scores ranged from 54 to 80 (M = 71.61, SD = 7.88); while the pre ASQ scores ranged from 20 to 70 (M = 44.35, SD = 10.26), and the post ASQ scores ranged from 35 to 70 (M = 53.7, SD = 10.36). In the TLM group, the pre CIS scores ranged from 48 to 80 (M = 67.86, SD = 7.61), and the post CIS scores ranged from 47 to 80 (M = 70.05, SD = 8.33); while the pre ASQ scores ranged from 30 to 90 (M = 52.14, SD = 18.14), and the post ASQ scores ranged from 25 to 80 (M = 47.86, SD = 16.92). In order to calculate if there was any increment amorg post-pre assessments, the score of each student's pre assessment was subtracted from the score of the post assessment. A positive number indicated an improvement after the four-week treatment period; otherwise, the number was equal to or less than zero. In the TBL group, the differences amorg the CIS post-pre assessments ranged from -9 to 16 (M = 1.39, SD =6.58), and the differences amorg the ASQ post-pre assessments ranged from -20 to 40 (M = 9.35, SD = 15.4). In the TLM group, the differences amorg the CIS post-pre assessments ranged from -15 to 27 (M = 2.19, SD = 9.99), and the differences amorg the ASQ post-pre assessments ranged from -35 to 35 (M = -4.29, SD = 16.98).	Overall results of data analysis Result and evidence

Paragraph 1 and ***paragraph 2*** state the demographic features of professor participants and student participants in order to guarantee the reliability and validity of the choice of the sample participants.

Paragraph 3 present the results of CIS and ASQ post-pre assessment for TBL and TLM groups. Also, this paragraph refers to how the data were analyzed and how the results were calculated. Besides mentioning the steps taken for analyzing and calculating the data, the author also explained the purpose behind the approach taken. Thus, we not only learn what the procedures were and what their purposes were but also learn more about how the steps were carried out. But, if the data provided in this paragraph can be demonstrated in a table by taking good use of a clear design of visual aid, then the results will be easier-to-read and more self-explanatory.

3) Results for Research Question 1

1. The following is a presentation of each research question included in this study. A one-way MANOVA, conducted by SPSS, was used to generate analyses in order to determine if there were statistically significant differences in student motivation and achievement between the two learning groups, TLM versus TBL, after the four-week treatment period.	Method
2. Q1. To what extent, if any, is there a difference in student motivation, as measured by the post-pre CIS, between the learning environment of TLM and TBL, among students in developmental mathematics courses at one community college in San Antonio, Texas? The corresponding null and alternative hypotheses were: as follows. H10: There is no significant difference in student motivation, as measured by the post-pre CIS, between the learning environment of TLM and TBL, among students in developmental mathematics courses. H1a: There is a significant difference in student motivation, as measured by the post-pre CIS, between the learning environment of TLM and TBL, among students in developmental mathematics courses.	Restate RQ and HP
3. The collected data were tested for presence of multicollinearity, normality of the distribution, and homogeneity of variances. Multicollinearity was tested by linear regression and the VIF = 1.005 was obtained. The VIF value was between 1 and 10; therefore, there was no multicollinearity (Lin, 2008). In order to test for normality of the distribution, a test for skewness and kurtosis was conducted, and the z-values were generated. The z-values for both skewness ($z = 0.77$) and kurtosis ($z = -0.14$) were between -1.96 and 1.96; therefore, it was assumed that the data were normally distributed. Homogeneity of variances was also verified by a Levene's test and $p = 0.06$ was obtained. The significant level was greater than 0.05; therefore, the null hypothesis was not rejected (Betz, 1987). An independent t-test was conducted to compare the pre CIS scores between the TLM and TBL groups.	Result and evidence Meaning Meaning

There was not a significant difference in the pre CIS scores for the TLM group (M = 67.86, SD = 7.61) and the TBL group (M = 70.22, SD = 8.18); t(42) = -0.99, p = 0.33 > 0.05. Therefore, the two groups had a similar measurement in motivation prior to the treatment.	Result and evidence Meaning
4. A one-way MANOVA was conducted after the statistical assumptions were tested. Twenty-one post-pre CIS entries were calculated from the TLM group (M = 2.19, SD = 9.99), while the number was 23 (M = 1.39, SD = 6.58) for the TBL group, as was shown in Figure 9.1. As a result, a total of 44 post-pre CIS responses (M = 1.77, SD = 8.29) were reported. The results of a one-way MANOVA showed that there was an overall significant multivariate main effect on learning environment, Wilk's = 0.84, F(2, 41) = 3.98, p = 0.03. However, the univariate main effects on motivation only indicated there was not a significant effect, F(1, 42) = 0.1, p = 0.75. Therefore, the null hypothesis, H_{10}, was not rejected. It was concluded that there was no significant difference in student motivation between the learning environment of TLM and TBL after the four-week treatment period.	Result and evidence Meaning

Figure 9.1 Comparison of Mean Post–pre CIS Scores

Having stated the preliminary data analysis result, we then presented the results that are relevant to research question 1. The first result to be reported in **paragraph 1** of this part is introduced with the statistical procedure that was used in the process. Then, in **paragraph 2**, the author restates the research questions and hypotheses for a more targeted explanation of the result. **Paragraph 3 and paragraph 4** are referred to the Figure 9.1 where the specific findings of the investigation are reported. The author also explains what these statistics mean in terms of statistical significance and statistical evidence. The author presents specific results and evidence before explaining what they actually mean, Then summarizes the key results of research question 1 by offering Figure 9.1. This is a clear and effective pattern. The summary at the end is particularly helpful for readers who may not have strong statistical knowledge. It also can show that the author fully understands what the results are saying.

Thus, this paragraph has restated the method and research question, introduced a result, explained how it was calculated, presented the statistical findings (with evidence) and commented on its degree of significance.

4) Results of Research Question 2

1. Q2. To what extent, if any, is there a difference in student achievement, as measured by the post-pre ASQ, between the learning environment of TLM and TBL, among students in developmental mathematics courses at one community college in San Antonio, Texas? The corresponding null and alternative hypotheses were as follows. H20: There is no significant difference in student achievement, as measured by the post-pre ASQ, between the learning environment of TLM and TBL, among students in developmental mathematics courses. H2a: There is a significant difference in student achievement, as measured by the post-pre ASQ, between the learning environment TLM and TBL, among students in developmental mathematics courses.	Restate RQ and HP
2. The collected data were tested for presence of multicollinearity, normality of the distribution, and homogeneity of variances. Multicollinearity was tested by linear regression and the VIF = 1.005 was obtained. The VIF value was between 1 and 10; therefore, there was no multicollinearity (Lin, 2008). In order to test for normality of the distribution, a test for skewness and kurtosis was conducted, and the z-values were generated. The z-values for both skewness (z = 0.41) and kurtosis (z = -0.66) were between -1.96 and 1.96; therefore, it was assumed that the data were normally distributed. Homogeneity of variances was also verified by a Levene's test and p = 0.92 was obtained. The significant level was greater than 0.05; therefore, the null hypothesis was not rejected (Betz, 1987). An independent t-test was conducted to compare the pre ASQ scores between the TLM and TBL groups. There was not a significant difference in the pre ASQ scores for the TLM group (M = 52.14, SD = 18.14) and the TBL	Result and evidence
group (M = 44.35, SD = 10.26), t (42) = 1.78, p = 0.08 > 0.05. Therefore, the two groups had a similar measurement in achievement prior to the treatment.	Meaning
3. A one-way MANOVA was conducted after the statistical assumptions were tested. Twenty-one post-pre ASQ entries were calculated from the TLM group (M = - 4.29, SD = 16.98), while the number was 23 (M = 9.34, SD = 15.4) for the TBL group, as was shown in Figure 9.2. As a result, a total of 44 post-pre ASQ responses (M = 2.84, SD = 17.4) were reported. The results of a one-way MANOVA showed that there was a significant univariate main effect, F(1, 42) = 7.81, p = 0.008. The	Result and evidence
	Meaning
null hypothesis, H20, was rejected because the results were statistically significant at the 0.05 level. It was concluded that there was a significant difference in student achievement between the learning environment of TLM and TBL after the four-week treatment period. As was shown in Figure 9.2, after the four-week treatment	Result and evidence
period, students in the TBL group showed a greater improvement in mathematics achievement, as measured by the post-pre ASQ, than the students in the TLM group.	Meaning
The average post ASQ score of the TBL group (M = 53.7, SD = 10.36) was higher than the average post ASQ score of the TLM group (M = 47.86, SD = 16.92).	Figure description

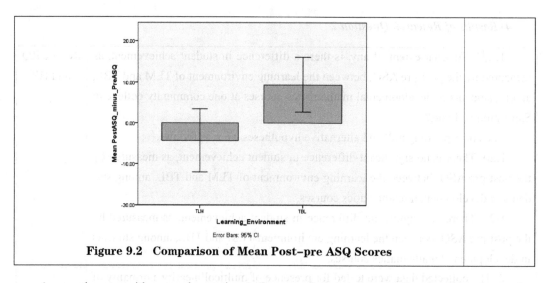

Figure 9.2   Comparison of Mean Post–pre ASQ Scores

As was the case with research question 1, ***Paragraph 1*** starts by restating the research question 2 and is followed up with the hypothesis under research question 2. In ***paragraph 2***, the results are presented for presence of multicollinearity, normality of the distribution, and homogeneity of variances, with evidence, an explanation of what they mean and with supporting evidence. ***Paragraph 3*** begins by stating that a one-way MANOVA was conducted after the statistical assumptions were tested. The findings are presented in Figure 9.2, as can be seen that the use of a figure makes the results so much more accessible for the reader. Figures are particularly helpful if there is a lot of statistical information in a particular finding. Evidence and explanation of results are considered in this paragraph. The author only draws the reader's attention to the results but does not interpret them or explain why they might have occurred, because these will be the focus of the discussion of a results chapter.

5) Summary

The purpose of this quantitative, ex post facto study was to examine the differences in individual student motivation and achievement in developmental mathematics courses as a result of incorporating TBL strategy as opposed to TLM strategy. The sample consisted of 44 students, who were enrolled in a developmental mathematics course in Fall 2015, at the community college in San Antonio, Texas.	Purpose of research
After the statistical assumptions were tested, a one-way MANOVA, conducted by SPSS, was used to generate analyses in order to determine if there were statistically significant differences in student motivation and achievement between the two learning groups, TLM versus TBL, after the four-week treatment period. The results indicated that there was not a significant difference in student motivation, as measured by the post-pre CIS, between the learning environment of TLM and TBL, among students in the developmental mathematics courses after the four-week	Sample description

treatment. The results further revealed that there was a significant difference in student achievement, as measured by the post-pre ASQ, between the learning environment of TLM and TBL, among students in the developmental mathematics courses after the four-week treatment.	Summary of results
The findings of the study were the first to reveal that the use of the specific learning strategy, the SLO, for four consecutive weeks did not have a significant effect on college students' motivation in the developmental mathematics courses. However, a significant difference in achievement was found between groups. Specifically, implementing the TBL strategy called the SLO, developed by the community college, resulted in a significant increase in student achievement. In addition, unlike	Summary of meaning of results
previous research conducted in multidisciplinary fields (Frame et al., 2015; Gray, 2014; Miller et al., 2015), the population of this study targeted specifically the college students, who were enrolled in developmental mathematics courses. Although students only spent 15 to 20 minutes weekly for four consecutive weeks engaging in the TBL activities, this short period of TBL engagement resulted in a significant increase in achievement. Even so, this engagement may not be enough time for students to demonstrate significant gain in motivation.	

The summary part is a conclusion of all the key findings of the research done. After restating the purpose of the study and a very brief description of samples, the author spent the next two paragraphs to conclude the result and the meaning of the result. If a reader would like to have a quick scan of the major findings of the research, the summary part can serve the purpose.

6) Some Linguistic Features of a Thesis Results Chapter

Hedging

It is also noteworthy that the author made extensive use of hedging. Hedging is a word or phrase whose job is to make things less fuzzy(Lakoff, 1973). This is understandable because of the limited number of items being referred to in the responses of the small number of participants. In doing so, the author can moderate observations in case further research of a quantitative nature reveals that the observations are not generalizable (Brett, 1994). The pragmatic functions of using hedging are as the following.

(1) *It covers the author's ignorance or insufficient knowledge in some aspect, hence, avoiding shouldering too many responsibilities.*

(2) *To be objective and avoids complete certainty.*

(3) *It helps the author avoid being too sure of something, thus helping to follow the politeness principle in verbal communication.*

This feature can be shown in the examples of this results chapter. The italicized parts of each sentence reveal the places where hedging has occurred.

e.g. These findings *suggest that* postmenopausal status *could be* a predisposing factor to declines in muscle strength, and *it is possible* that this relation could be mediated, at least in part, by the increased incidence of SDB among this subgroup.

e.g. Therefore, *it was assumed* that the data were normally distributed.

e.g. Even so, this engagement *may not* be enough time for students to demonstrate significant gain in motivation.

Presenting Results Visually

There is much that can be said about the use of tables and figures, and even more that can be said about those that are created to reveal the findings of particular types of statistical testing(Yang & Allison, 2003). There are plenty of books available that you can consult for how to make good use of tables and figures to better illustrate data. There are some general guidelines for the visual representation of your results(Cooley & Lewkowicz, 2003).

(1) *There are different opinions about whether to compare values down columns or across rows. The key point is consistency in approach throughout your thesis.*

(2) *Avoid any attempt to put every detail in a table. Be selective so that the focus is clear for the reader. Visual appeal and clarity is a key consideration.*

(3) *A clear relationship amorg tables, figures and text is essential. There must be a clear connection of what is presented in the table, what is presented in a figure and the use of language. For example, if you are referring to a particular measure or scale with a particular designation, the same designation must be used in all tables, figures and text.*

(4) *Use appropriate labels for each form of visual representation and make sure they are not too long. Avoid abbreviations unless they have been clearly introduced in preceding text or arc supplied in notes at the foot of the visual representation.*

(5) *Consult the most recent style manual for guidelines on the components of a table and figure, numbering, titles, headings, body and notes.*

9.5 Discussion of Results

In this chapter, we will be considering the discussion of results as a separate chapter from the presentation of results and conclusion chapters, though some theses combine the discussion of results and conclusions in one chapter. Considering now the discussion of results as a single chapter, we begin with a consideration of the purpose and functions of the chapter before looking at the content and structure that might be considered. The chapter will again conclude with a discussion of some key linguistic features of discussion chapters.

9.5.1 The Functions of a Thesis Discussion of Results

The key purpose of this chapter is to discuss the meaning and significance of the results or findings of the research. Consequently, the discussion will have a number of functions, which are shown below (Bitchener, 2018).

(1) *The discussionis an overview of the aims of the research that refers to the research questions or hypotheses.*

(2) *The discussionis a summary of the theoretical and research contexts of the study.*

(3) *The discussionis a summary of the methodological approach.*

(4) *The discussionis about the contribution made to the research questions and therefore to existing theory, research and practice (i.e. their importance and significance).*

(5) *This discussion will often include an interpretation of the results, a comparison with other research, an explanation of why the results occurred and an evaluation of the contribution to the field of knowledge.*

9.5.2 The Content and Structure of a Thesis Discussion of Results

The following content units provide a number of options to consider when deciding how to discuss your results. They should not be seen as a prescriptive list that should be presented in this order. The extent to which the sample thesis has employed these options and recycled them is the focus of the next section. The following table (which has been introduced in Chapter 7) lists the content units for writing this chapter (Bitchener, 2018).

Main units	sub−units
1. Provide any background information considered important for understanding the discussion.	a. Restate aim (s), research questions/hypotheses, key research and methodological approach.
2. Present a statement of result.	a. Restate a key result.
	b. Expand statement about the key result.
3. Evaluate/comment on each result.	a. Explain the result by suggesting reasons for it.
	b. Explain whether the result was expected or unexpected.
	c. Compare the result with the results of previous research.
	d. Provide exampces of the result.
	e. Make a more general claim arising from the result, draw a conclusion or state a hypothesis.
	f. Quote previous research to support.
	g. Make suggestions forfur ther research.
	h. Justify why further research is recommended.

9.5.3 Sample Analysis of a Thesis Discussion of Results

The author of our sample thesis discusses the results focusing on the two research questions that guided the study. In this section, we will consider the content units that used in the discussion of research questions.

1) Introduction

> **Introduction**
>
> This chapter will discuss implications, recommendations for practical application and future research, and conclusions. First, the implications of the study will be discussed based on the study results and how they are related to the current literature. Afterward, recommendations for practical application and future research will be discussed. The conclusions will be provided at the end of this chapter.

Like previous chapter introductions, this one also provides an advance organization of what is to be presented in the chapter. The author begins by explaining that her discussion will be organized around the two research questions and that it will focus on the implication and recommendation of the research.

2) Implication

Implications 1. The implications of the findings will be discussed along with the presentation of the two research questions used in this quantitative, ex post facto study. The findings represented a contribution to current knowledge regarding how learning environment could affect student motivation and achievement in developmental mathematics courses. The findings also contributed to current knowledge of the SDT and the ARCSMMD. Each research question will be presented along with a brief review and followed by the implications of the research question.	Structure of this part
2. Q1. To what extent, if any, is there a difference in student motivation, as measured by the post-pre CIS, between the learning environment of TLM and TBL, among students in developmental mathematics courses at one community college in San Antonio, Texas?	Restatement of RQ
3. The two learning environment, TBL and TLM, did not have a significant effect on student motivation in the developmental mathematics courses. It was expected that students in the TBL group would show a significant improvement in the level of motivation, as measured by the post-pre CIS, compared with the TLM group. The lack of a significant difference in motivation between the two learning groups could imply that the current teaching method used in the developmental mathematics courses may be sufficient to maintain student motivation. Nevertheless, the implication of the results contradicted literature and the ARCSMMD, which revealed an increased students' motivation as a result of an incorporation of student-centered social TBL strategy (Burks, 2011; Karoulis, 2011; Meepian & Wannapiroon, 2013; Woo, 2014; Yuretich & Kanner, 2015). Unlike results found in other disciplinary studies; the findings of this study were the first to reveal that the four-week treatment did not significantly affect college students' level of	Explanation and expansion of research result Explanation and expansion of research result

motivation in the developmental mathematics courses. The ARCSMMD posits that students' motivation is increased when they feel accomplished and acquire new knowledge from a learning task (Kim, 2012). Studies have shown that an incorporation of non-traditional teaching strategies resulted in a higher level of motivation in learning (Karoulis, 2011; Lee, 2012; Woo, 2014). *Nevertheless, the findings of this study may imply that an incorporation of TBL strategy may not be effective to increase student motivation in mathematics courses.*	Implication
4. Previous research indicated that the majority of college students favored the TBL method of learning and showed a higher level of course satisfaction, compared with TLM (Yuretich & Kanner, 2015). Nevertheless, these results have been inconsistent because students, who learned in the TBL learning environment, negatively assessed this teaching method for they experienced a higher stress level (Miller, Falcone & Metz, 2015). In order to finish each SLO, students in this study were required to work as a team, discuss each question, and generate an answer agreed by all team members. Students in the TBL group showed a lower improvement in the level of motivation compared with the TLM group. The results may imply that utilizing these TBL activities in a mathematics course may not be an effective method to increase student motivation (Gray et al., 2014; Miller et al., 2015).	Previous Study Implication
5. The limitations of this study may be the reasons that there was not a significant difference between groups. For example, the frequency of TBL implementation was a limitation, and it has been shown that students, who had more time to become familiar with a TBL environment, were more likely to have positive perceptions about the learning strategy (Frame, 2015). For standardization without altering the curriculum requirements, the SLO was implemented once a week for four consecutive weeks during the 95-minute class time. Therefore, the findings may imply that this limitation could have influenced the results. In addition, the data gathered from the post-pre CIS should be interpreted with caution because participants in both groups started and ended with high CIS scores. For that reason, it was suspected that the ceiling effect could be the reason that a significant difference between groups could not be established. Based on an a priori power analysis, this study required at least 42 students altogether. Although invitations were sent to 120 students, who were enrolled in the developmental mathematics courses in Fall 2015, only 44 participants, in which 21 students were in the TLM group and 23 students were in the TBL group, completed both pre and post assessments. Therefore, although a ceiling effect was observed, there were not enough entries so that extreme scores could be excluded. This limitation may imply that a larger data set was needed.	Limitation of the research

Paragraph 1 presents an outline of this part, followed by ***paragraph 2*** with a restatement of research question 1. An explanation and illustration of the result for RQ 1 is presented with a short

expansion in ***paragraph 3***. In presenting the first group of illustrations, implications of the result are also offered in the same paragraph. Then, previous research was referred to in order to support the explanation being given in ***paragraph 4***. And by comparing the research result with the resuct of previous research, more implications and new perspectives of the result were indicated. As a result of these illustrations of the statement of the result, further claims are made and these are supported with reference to previous research. The extent to which the results were expected or unexpected in light of previous research is then considered. The author considers the research that the results do not support and, in doing so, offers some explanations. The discussion closes with a limitation of the present research which lists four aspects of limitations which need further improvement.

The author then moves on to discuss the results for the second research question. Because the approach taken for research question 2 is the same, we will skip that part and focus our attention on the part of the recommendations.

3) Recommendation

Recommendations 1. The results in this study suggested that the four-week treatment of TBL did not significantly affect students' motivation in the developmental mathematics courses compared with the students in the TLM group. On the other hand, a significant difference in achievement was revealed between the two learning groups. Based on the findings from this current study, recommendations for practical application and future research are presented below.	Introduction to recommendation
Recommendations for Practical Application 2. This present study was the first to reveal that students, who experienced the four-week TBL strategies in the developmental mathematics courses, improved significantly on achievement in comparison with the TLM group. Nevertheless, the treatment did not have a significant effect on student motivation.	Recommendation
3. An incorporation of the socially interactive, student-centered TBL has been shown to result in a great number of benefits (Brandon & All, 2010). For example, learners constructed knowledge in a contextualized process and became independent learners; they also had the opportunity to be engaged in learning activities and gained confidence and motivation in learning (Denton, 2012; Jia, 2010; Savasci & Berlin, 2012). In this study, the specific TBL activity designed by the community college called the SLO was implemented in the TBL group. One of the instructions to complete the SLO was that the instructors do not teach the students directly when they asked for help. Instead, instructors should elaborate and guide the group toward solving the problems successfully. Students' achievement in the TBL group increased significantly. For this reason, it is recommended that teachers in student-centered learning	Previous research Exemplification Explanation

environment act as facilitators, who promote self-regulated learning, so that students can construct new knowledge based on the learning experiences. *Although there was not a significant difference in motivation, a significant difference was found in achievement between the two learning groups, TBL and TLM.* Findings have shown that 71% of students agreed that an engagement in student-centered TBL increased	Restatement of Result

Exemplification and support from |
their knowledge and ability of fundamental skills in mathematics (Burks, 2011). Therefore, it is recommended that the specific SLO be used as a supplement in mathematics courses.	previous research
4. TBL is becoming one of the popular teaching strategies used in mathematics classrooms. Nevertheless, traditional teaching strategies are still favored by a great number of teachers (Mullins et al., 2014). Instructors expressed that, on average, the amount of time teachers needed to prepare a well-planned student-centered learning environment was more than planning traditional teaching activities (R. E. Allen et al., 2013). Teachers expressed that the lack of preparation time was one of the reasons why traditional methods remained popular in the twenty-first century (Berrett, 2012; H. Friedman & L. Friedman, 2011; Sturgis, 2012).	Support from previous research
5. In this study, participating professors did not have to spend any time preparing for the TBL activities because the SLO assignments were delivered to them weekly. Therefore, it is recommended that schools and districts curriculum writers provide predesigned TBL activities to teachers so that they are more willing to implement those activities. In addition, professional development should be conducted for teachers, so that they are familiar with the purposes, procedures, expectations, and goals of implementing TBL activities in their classes. Students pointed out that instructional activities involving TBL imposed a significant amount of pressure, self-regulation, and responsibilities on them, especially when learning new content or abstract concepts (Boonlerts & Inprasitha, 2013; Miller et al., 2015).	Recommendation for classroom teaching and learning
6. Student participants in this study only engaged in four simple TBL activities for 15 to 20 minutes per week, and the results still indicated a significant improvement in achievement. Furthermore, students also had the opportunities to reflect on what they learned and received instant feedback from their peers and instructor in the process of completing each activity. It has been shown that maintaining communication and exchanging feedback among teachers and students helped sustain student success (Shillingford & Karlin, 2013; Woo, 2014). Thus, an incorporation of short TBL activities that are simple yet relevant to the curriculum may be sufficient for students to improve their achievement.	Recommendation for classroom teaching and learning

7. Although implanting TBL strategies is not a requirement for professors at the study side, it is recommended for them to use SLO activities because students' achievement increased based on the post-pre ASQ scores. In order to increase student motivation, it is recommended that professors be provided with a different TBL activity because the implementation of the SLO did not increase student motivation, as measured by the post-pre CIS. Staff development is encouraged, so that professors understand the purpose, goals, and expectation of TBL activities.	Reinforcement on the recommendation above
Recommendations for Future Research 8. Based on a four-week research period conducted in the local community college in Texas, the findings indicated that the learning environment, TBL or TLM, did not have a significant effect on student motivation, but it had a significant effect on student achievement in mathematics. However, this present study had several limitations; therefore, the following are the recommendations for future research.	Recommendation based on limitations
9. First, time and financial limitations made it unpractical to conduct research for all college students in America (Krathwohl, 1998; Mason, 1996). Therefore, the sample only included 44 students, who were enrolled in a local community college in Texas. In this region, 74% of the participants identified themselves as Hispanic, and 77% of the participants were female. Furthermore, the teaching strategies were delivered only by professors, who were at least 46 years old. For these reasons, it is recommended for future research to involve a more diverse population from different geographical regions in the U.S.	Limitation Exemplification Recommendation
10. Second, although demographic questionnaires, which included age, gender, and ethnicity, were conducted as a part of the CIS, a cross subgroup comparison was not executed in this present study.	Same as Para.9
11. Third, the frequency of TBL implementation was a limitation of this study.	Same as Para.9
12. One of the goals of this research was to improve mathematics education and educational outcome in the U.S. Therefore, future research could examine student motivation and achievement related to different types of TBL activities in mathematics classes. In addition, future studies could assess different components of TBL, such as duration, frequency, and complexity, and their effectiveness on student motivation and achievement. Furthermore, the participants of this study only included students, who were enrolled in developmental mathematics courses at one community college. Thus, future research could extend to students, who take mathematics courses at a different level, such as K-12 students and postgraduates. A mixed design that includes qualitative data, such as student interviews, is recommended for future research because a qualitative approach may be used to provide in depth attitudes and ideas of an individual toward engaging in TBL activities (Vogt, 2007).	Research goal Recommendations

Paragraph 1 is the introduction paragraph which begins with the restatement of the result findings presented in the results chapter and indicates that the recommendation will be given on practical application and future research.

Paragraph 2~7 are the recommendations for practical application. Paragraph 2~4 revealed a cyclic pattern of content units in response to a statement of the result. Explanation, previous research and exemplification were most frequently employed. Arising from the discussion, the author identifies further recommendations for professors and students in classroom teaching in paragraph 5 and 6. Then, paragraph 7 concluded this part by reinforcing the recommendation above.

Paragraph 8~12 states the recommendations for future research. Paragraph 8 is an introduction paragraph indicating that the recommendations for future research are given on the basis of the limitations of the research. Paragraph 9 stated time and financial limitation first and then referred to the exemplification from the research results and offered the relevant recommendation. Paragraph 10 and 11 used the same pattern as the structure: limitation — exemplification — recommendation. Again, we can see the cyclic nature of the content structure of the discussion of the recommendation of future research. Paragraph 12 ended this part by references to the research goals and implied five hypotheses that might be tested in further research.

4) Conclusion

Conclusions	
1. The purpose of this quantitative, ex post facto study was to examine the differences in individual student motivation and achievement in developmental mathematics courses as a result of incorporating TBL strategy as opposed to TLM strategy. The problem addressed in this study was that approximately 70% of high school students, who graduated, enrolled in postsecondary education (Baum et al., 2013). Nevertheless, benchmark of 2011 showed that only 45% of high school graduates were college-ready and only 60% of those students completed a degree-seeking program (Clagett, 2013; Goldstein et al., 2011). The other 55% of students, who were not college ready, had to take one or more mathematics courses at the developmental level. Even with the assistance and training they had received in developmental courses, approximately three-fourths of those students still could not successfully complete a college-leveled mathematics course (Bahr, 2013; Fain, 2012). Consequently, less than 50% of those students had graduated from college. It has been shown that ineffectiveness of instructional strategies could be one factor that led to low completion rates in developmental mathematics courses (Yuksel, 2010). For instance, using a TLM strategy on students in the twenty-first century did not improve their motivation toward learning or academic achievement (Nafees et al., 2012; Young, 2009). On the other hand, the incorporation of TBL strategies increased student motivation and academic performance in multiple disciplinary studies	Restatement of purpose of research

(Hsiung, 2012; Wong & Abbruzzese, 2011; Yuretich & Kanner, 2015). Therefore, there was a need to measure the differences in individual student motivation and achievement in developmental mathematics courses as a result of incorporating TLM versus TBL.	
2. In this current study, the univariate main effects obtained with a one-way MANOVA indicated a nonsignificant difference in student motivation, as measured by the post-pre CIS, between the learning environment of TLM and TBL, among students in the developmental mathematics courses after the four-week treatment. On the contrary, these results further indicated a significant difference in student achievement, as measured by the post-pre ASQ, between the learning environment of TLM and TBL, among students in the developmental mathematics courses after the four-week treatment. The findings of this study were the first to reveal that the four-week treatment did not significantly affect college students' level of motivation in developmental mathematics courses. However, a significant difference was found in achievement between the two learning groups. The results may imply that utilizing TBL activities in a mathematics course may not be an effective method to increase student motivation (Gray et al., 2014; Miller et al., 2015). The findings may further imply that SLO activities for 15 to 20 minutes could be used as an effective supplement to an existing curriculum, and those activities can still help improve college students' achievement in developmental mathematics courses.	Restatement of Results
3. TBL is becoming one of the most popular teaching strategies used in mathematics classrooms. Nevertheless, traditional teaching strategies are still favored by a great number of teachers and students (Mullins et al., 2014). The concern with this instructional method was that it took a long time for teachers to prepare and for students to finish a TBL activity (Berrett, 2012; H. Friedman & L. Friedman, 2011; Mowatt, 2010; Sturgis, 2012). Therefore, it is recommended that predesigned TBL activities be provided for teachers so that they are more willing to implement those activities. In addition, teachers should limit each TBL activity to 15 to 20 minute and use it weekly as a part of curriculum. Improving mathematics education and educational outcome in the U.S. was a purpose of this research. Therefore, future research should examine different types of TBL activities in mathematics classes and different components of TBL, such as duration, frequency, and complexity, and their effectiveness on student motivation and achievement.	Restatement of discussion and recommedantion

Often than not, authors like to put conclusion part in the discussion part. This conclusion is an overall summary of all the essence of the study, with paragraph 1 on the purpose of study, paragraph 2 on the result and paragraph 3 on the discussion and recommendations. The summary has therefore drawn the readers' attention to the key contribution that the study has made to existing knowledge (theory, research and practice). The significance of the findings and this discussion will be highlighted in the conclusions that the author offers in the concluding chapter.

9.5.4 Some Linguistic Features of a Thesis Discussion of Results

As you discuss the significance of your findings, there will be occasions when you can be quite assertive about the significance and contribution of your findings to the field you are working within and occasions when you need to be more tentative in the claims that you make (Hewings, 1993). While care needs to be taken, you should not shy away from claiming that a particular finding supports or does not support existing research and knowledge if it does. In the discussion chapter, you will seek to account for particular findings. If you are presenting possibilities rather than absolute certainties, you need to make sure that you hedge in your presentation of them (Thompson, 2005). In the previous chapter, we referred to various ways in which hedging can be achieved. As an example of how this can be achieved in the discussion chapter, consider the extensive use of hedging approaches that have been used in the following paragraph from the sample thesis discussion.

cant effect on student motivation in the developmental mathematics courses. It was expected that students in the TBL group would show a significant improvement in the level of motivation, as measured by the post-pre CIS, compared with the TLM group. The lack of a significant difference in motivation between the two learning groups could imply the two learning environment, TBL and TLM, did not have a signifi that the current teaching method used in the developmental mathematics courses may be sufficient to maintain student motivation. Nevertheless, the findings of this study may imply that an incorporation of TBL strategy may not be effective to increase student motivation in mathematics courses.	Hedge verb Modal verb Modal verb Modal verb Modal verb

In another example from the sample thesis, consider the author's willingness to be up front and assertive in the sentence below.

Previous research indicated that the majority of college students favored the TBL method of learning and showed a higher level of course satisfaction, compared with TLM (Yuretich & Kanner, 2015). Nevertheless, these results have been inconsistent because students, who learned in the TBL learning environment, negatively assessed this teaching method because they experienced a higher stress level.

9.6 Abstract

The abstracts is an important part of reports and research papers. It is often the last item you write, but the first part people read when they want to have a quick overview of the entire paper. It is a short, self-contained, powerful summary of an article, paper or thesis. It is the miniature version of the paper. Usually the length of an abstract is about 300 words. This chapter will look at the type of content that may be included in a thesis abstract and how the content can be organized. But first, we need to consider the purpose or function of an abstract. Then, focuses will be put on the content areas typically included in a thesis abstract and on the ways in which this material may be presented effectively. Analysis of an abstract written by a doctoral student will be provided in the chapter(Ku, 2016). This will be followed up with a discussion of one of the key linguistic features of abstracts.

9.6.1 The Functions of a Thesis Abstract

The key aim of a thesis abstract is to introduce the reader to the main considerations of the thesis so most often include the following functions (Bitchener, 2018).

(1) The aims of the study.

(2) The background and context of the study.

(3) The methodology and methods used in the study.

(4) The key findings of the study.

(5) The contribution of the study to the field of knowledge.

To some extent, it also has a persuasive function, namely, convincing readers that the main text has something new and important to offer. Next, how both the content and its organization are determined by the functions of an abstract will be presented.

9.6.2 The Content and Ttructure of a Thesis Abstract

In this section, we are going to consider the content units and sub-units that can be used when writing a thesis abstract, which has been mentioned in chapter 7 (Bitchener, 2018).

Main units	Sub-units
1. Introduction	a. Outline background, context of the study.
	b. Explain the motivation for the research.
	c. Explain the significance and centrality of the research focus.
	d. Identify the knowledge gap(s) or need for the continuation of a tradition.
2. Purpose	a. Identify the aims or intentions, research questions/hypotheses.
	b. Develop aspects of (a).
3. Method	a. Identify and justify the methodological approach and methods.
	b. Identify key design aspects.
	c. Identify data sources.
	d. Identify data analysis processes.
4. Product	a. Present main findings of research questions/hypotheses.
5. Conclusion	a. Suggest significance/importance of the findings to the field.
	b. Identify any important limitations.
	c. Make recommendations for further research.

So, from the table above, we can see that an abstract is a miniature of the whole thesis, which mainly consists of the introduction, the methodology, the result and the discussion of the thesis. By reading an abstract, a reader can get the essence of the study in a brief way. However, how to use these content units may vary from topic to topic. When we analyze the abstract from the sample thesis in the next section, you will see that the author included most of the content units.

9.6.3 Analysis of a Thesis Abstract

In this section, we will be analyzing the abstract from the sample thesis.

Abstract	
1. Obtaining a degree from a community college could be the opportunity for students to advance their education or career. Nevertheless, nearly two-thirds of first-time community college students in the U.S. are required to take developmental mathematics courses. The problem is that approximately three-fourths of those students do not successfully complete a mathematics course at college level, despite the assistance and training in developmental mathematics courses. Therefore, the purpose of this quantitative, ex post facto study is to examine the differences in individual student motivation and achievement in developmental mathematics courses after incorporating team-based learning (TBL) strategy as opposed to traditional learning model (TLM).	Introduction—background Introduction—research gap Introduction—purpose of research
2. Invitations were sent to 120 students, who were enrolled in a three-hour credit developmental mathematics course in Fall 2015 at a community college in San Antonio, Texas. Forty-four results were analyzed, in which 21 were from the TLM group and 23 were from the TBL group. Participating professors completed the Teaching Style Inventory to determine their teaching style. Team-based professors incorporated the TBL activities once a week for four consecutive weeks. Participating students completed the Course Interest Survey, to assess their motivation reaction to specific instructional environment, and the ACCUPLACER Sample Questions, to measure their achievement before and after the treatment.	Methodology—participants Methodology—design
3. The results of a one-way MANOVA showed that there was an overall significant main effect on learning environment, $F(2, 41)= 3.98, p < 0.03$. However, while there was no significant main effect on motivation, $F(1, 42) = 0.1, p = 0.75$, there was a significant main effect on achievement, $F(1, 42) = 7.81, p = 0.008$. Therefore, there has been no significant difference in motivation; nevertheless, there has been a significant difference in achievement.	Results—data explanation Results—explanation
4. These results implied that the incorporation of the TBL strategy could be used to increase student achievement, but not motivation in mathematics courses. It was recommended that simply predesigned TBL activities be provided so that teachers and students may be more willing to implement and complete those activities. Moreover, future research should examine different types of TBL activities and components and their effectiveness on student motivation and achievement in mathematics classes.	Implication and Recommendation

Paragraph 1 introduces the wider context of the study and points to its importance as a central area of current research interest. Although it is a very general, introductory statement, it draws our attention to the existing problem that three-fourths of those students did not successfully complete a mathematics course at college level. Then this paragraph explains the central purpose of this ongoing investigation, namely examining the differences in individual student motivation and achieve-

ment in developmental mathematics courses after incorporating team-based learning (TBL) strategy as opposed to traditional learning model (TLM). So, this introduction paragraph has revealed about the background, the research gap and the purpose of the study.

Paragraph 2 is a methodology paragraph which begins with a description of participants. Student participants are divided into TLM group and TBL group. Teacher participants who are differentiated by Teaching Style Inventory are required to carry out different teaching methods on the two groups of students. And then this paragraph explains the design of the study and the way of collecting data briefly.

Paragraph 3 illustrates mainly the results from a one-way MANOVA by offering the major findings from the analysis of the data collected. Then, based on the analysis, some direct explanation is given.

Paragraph 4 is the discussion paragraph which states the significance of the study by offering the implications and recommendations respectively.

9.6.4 Linguistic Feature of a Thesis Abstract

Tense

One of the most important linguistic features to note when writing an abstract is the use of the appropriate tense (Blog, 2004). Because an abstract is reporting what has been done in the study that is about to be reported on, is contextualizing the study in the existing literature and/or is commenting on the extent of the study's contribution to that context, different verb tenses are required to convey these various details(Kaplan, Cantor, Hagstrom, Shiotani & Zimmerman, 1994). The table below identifies examples from the abstract of the sample thesis to illustrate the usage of three different tenses. It should also be noted though that there may be some choice in the use of tense on some occasions. For example, although the author has used the past simple tense to convey the point that practical implications and future research suggestions were identified, other authors may have chosen to use the present tense (Salager-Mayer, 1990).

Tense	Example	Function
The present simple tense	*The problem is that approximately three-fourths of those students do not successfully complete a mathematics course at college level.*	Description of background such as the comment, the discussion, the report, knowledge, the research
The past simple tense	*Forty-four results were analyzed, in which 21 were from the TLM group and 23 were from the TBL group.*	Work done
The present perfect	*Therefore, there has been no significant difference in motivation; nevertheless, there has been a significant difference in achievement.*	Stress the influence brought by research

Sentence Patterns in the Abstract

1) Introduce the Research

Verbs: consider, discuss, investigate, study, etc.

- This article discusses the reasons for… and offers an insight into…
- This paper analyzes some important characteristics of…
- The paper examines…and considers…
- The author considers two specific subjects which…
- A principle of constructing … is considered in the paper.
- The influence of …on … is investigated.
- The process is analyzed using…
- The performance characteristics of …are studied theoretically and experimentally.

2) State the Purpose

Verbs: aim, intend, seek, etc

- One of the purposes of this study is …
- This paper seeks to justify…in terms of…
- The aim of this study is to carry out analysis for…
- The study is intended to…

3) Describe the Method

- The formula is derived from…
- The test is demonstrated by using…
- The analysis was made with…

4) Outline Chief Result

Verbs: find, result in, etc.

- It is found/indicated that …
- It was found/observed between/in…
- The results of statistically elaborated computations are tabulated.

5) Discussion and Recommendations

Verbs: propose, recommend to, suggest, etc.

- The data/results/solutions obtained suggest that…
- Recommendations are made regarding…
- Suggestions were made for further study of…
- The author proposes an approach to…

References

Andrews R. (1995). *Teaching and Learning Argument.* London, NY: Cassell.

Behrens L., Rosen L. J. & Beedles B. (2004). *Sequence for Academic Writing* (2nd ed.). New York: Pearson.

Bitchener J. (2010). *Writing an Applied Linguistics Thesis or Dissertation: A Guide to Presenting Empirical Research*. Houndsmill, UK: Palgrave Macmillan.

Bitchener J. (2018). *A Guide to Supervising Non-native English Wrtiers of Thesis and Dissertations*. New York: Routledge.

Blog K. (2004). How to Write an Abstract for a Research Paper. https://www.kibin.com/essay-writing-blog/how-to-write-an-abstract-for-a-research-paper/ website.

Brett P. (1994). A Genre Analysis of the Results Sections of Sociology Articles. *English for Special Purposes, 13*, 47~59.

Brown A., Iwashita N. & McNamara T. (2005). An Examination of Rater Orientations and Test-taker Performance on English-for-Academic-Purposes Speaking Tasks. In *TOEFL Monograph Series MS-29*. Princeton, NJ: Educational Testing Service.

Bruce I. (2008). Cognitive Genre Structures in Methods Secitons of Research Articles: A Corpus Study. *Journal of English for Academic Purposes, 7*, 38~54.

Bunton D. (2002). Generic Moves in PhD Thesis Introductions. In J. Flowerdew (Ed.), *Academic Discourse*. London: Longman.

Burdick A. (1990). Faithful Witness: The Empirical Method Intrudes on Medieval Medicine. *The Science*(January — February).

Carmel H., Huang M. & Tam M. K. (2007). *Art of Academic Writing*. Singapore: Pearson Custom Publishing.

Carter R. & McCarthy M. (2006). *Cambridge Grammar of English*. Cambridge: Cambridge University Press.

Clark S. & Pointon G. *A Guide to Academic Writing for Students*. Oxon: Routledge.

Cooley L. & Lewkowicz J. (2003). *Dissertation Writing in Practice: Turning Ideas into Text*. Hong Kong: Hong Kong University Press.

Ding W. D., Wu B., Zhong M. S. & Guo Q. Q. (2009). *A Handbook of Writing*. Beijing: Foreign Language Teaching and Research Press.

DÖrnyei Z. (2007). *Research Methods in Applied Linguistics*. Oxford: Oxford University Press.

Ellis R. & Yuan F. (2004). The Effects of Planning on Fluency, Complexity, and Accuracy in Second Language Narrative Writing. *Studies in Second Language Acquisition, 26*, 59–84.

Evans D. & Gruba P. (2002). *How to Write a Better Thesis*. Melbourne, Australia: Melbourne University Press.

Galvan J. (2009). *Writing Literature Review: A Guid for Students of the Social and Behaviorual Sciences*. Glaendale, CA: Pyrezak Publishing.

Hagberg G. (1977-). *Philosophy and Literature*. United States: Johns Hopkins University Press.

Hart C. (1998). *Doing a Literature Review*. London: Sage.

Hart C. (2005). *Doing your Masters Dissertation*. London: Sage.

Hewings M. (1993). The end! How to Conclude a Dissertation. In G. Blue (Ed.), *Language, Learning and Success: Studying Through English*. London: Modern Publications in Association with the British Council, Macmillan.

Huddleston R. (1984). *Introduction to the Grammar of English*. Cambridge: Cambridge University Press.

Hughes R. (1996). *English in Speech and writing: Investigating language and Literature*. London: Routledge.

Hundt M. & Mair C. (1999). "Agile" and "Uptight" Genres: The Corpus-based Approach to Language Change in Progress. *International Journal of Corpus Linguistics, 4*, 221~242.

Hurley M., Dennett D. C. & Adams, R. B. (2011). *Inside Jokes: Using Humor to ReVerse-engineer the Mind*. London: The MIT Press.

Hyland K. (2000). *Disciplinary Discourses: Social Interactions in Academic Writing*. London: Longman.

Kaplan R., Cantor S., Hagstrom C., Shiotani Y. & Zimmerman C. (1994). On Abstract Writing. *Text, 14*, 401~426.

Ku J. Y. F. (2016). *A Quantitative Study Examining the Differences in Motivation and Achievement Between Traditional Versus Team-based Learning*. (Doctor of philosophy), Northcentral University, Prescott Valley, Arizona.

Lakoff G. (1973). Hedges: A Study in Meaning Criteria and the Logic of Fuzzy Concepts. *Journal of Philosophical Logic, 2*(4), 458-508.

Larsen-Freeman D. (2006). The Emergence of Complexity, Fluency, and Accuracy in the Oral and Written Production of Five Chinese Learners of English. *Applied Linguistics, 27*, 590~619.

Leech G., Hundt M., Mair C. & Smith N. (2009). *Change in Contemporary English: A Grammatical Study*. Cambridge: Cambridge University Press.

Li Y. L. (2000). Linguistic Characteristics of ESL Writing in Task-based E-mail Activities. *System, 28*, 229~245.

Lucas S. (2007). *The Art of Public Speaking* Beijing: Foreign Language Teaching and Research Press.

Mackey A. & Gass S. (2005). *Second Language Research: Methodology and Design*. Mahwah, NJ: Lawrence Erlbaum Associates.

Mair C. (2006). *Twentieth-century English: History, Variation and Standardization*. Cambridge: Cambridge University Press.

McWhorter J. (2001). *The Word on the Street: Debunking the Myth of "Pure" Standard English*. New York: Basic Books.

Moskovsky C., Alrabai F., Paolini S. & Ratcheva S. (2013). The Effects of Teachers' Motivational Strategies on Learners' Motivation: A Controlled Investigation of Second Language Acquisition. *Language Learning, 63*(1), 34~62.

Moss A. & Holder C. (1988). *Improving Student Writing: A Guide for Faculty in All Disci-

plines. Dubuque, IA: Kendll/Hunt.

Murray C. (1993). The Coming White Underclass. *Wall Street Journal*.

Nelson N. & Van Meter A. (2007). Measuring Written Langauge Ability in Narrative Samples. *Reading and Writing Quarterly, 23*(3), 287~309.

Norrby C. & Hakansson G. (2007). The Interaction of Complexity and Grammatical Processability: The Case of Swedish as a Foreign Language. *International Review of Applied Linguistics, 45*, 45~68.

Okin S. M. (1999). *Is Multiculturalism Bad for Women?* Princeton: Princeton University Press.

Paltridge B. & Starfield, S. (2007). *Thesis and Dissertation Writing in a Second Language: A Handbook for Supervisors*. New York: Routledge.

Pinker S. (2014). Why Academics Stink at Writing *The Chronicle Review*.

Purpura J. (2004). *Assessing Grammar*. Cambridge: Cambridge University Press.

Rifkin J. (1998). The Ultimate Therapy: Commercial Eugenics on the Eve of the Biotech Century. *Tikkun*(May-June), 35.

Rudestam K. & Newton R. (2001). *Surviving Your Dissertation: A Comprehensive Guide to Content and Process*. Newbury Park, CA: Sage.

Ryan R. M. & Deci E. L. (2000). Intrinsic and Extrinsic Motivations: Classics Definitions and New Directions. *Contemporary Educational Psychology, 25*, 54~67.

Salager-Mayer F. (1990). Discoursal Flaws in Medical English Abstracts: A Genre Analysis per Research and Text Type. *Text, 10*, 365~384.

Seliger H. & Shohamy E. (1989). *Second Language Research Methods*. Cambridge: Cambridge University Press.

Starr C. & Taggart R. (1998). Recombinant DNA and Genetic Engineering In *Biology: The Unity and Diversity of Life* (pp. 133). New York: Wadsworth.

Swales J. M. (2004). *Research Genres: Explorations and Applications*. Cambridge: Cambridge University Press.

Swales J. M. & Feak C. (2004). *Academic Writing for Graduate Students*. Ann Arbor: University of Michigan Press.

Thompson p. (2005). Points of Focus and Position: Intertextual Reference in PhD Theses. *Journal of English for Academic Purposes, 4*, 307~323.

Toulmin S., Reike R. & Janik A. (1984). *An Introduction to reasoning*. New York: Macmillan.

Wikipedia. https://en.wikipedia.org/wiki/Structure_of_the_Earth.

Willis D. (2003). *Rules, Patterns and Words: Grammar and Lexis in English Language Teaching*. Cambridge: Cambridge University Press.

Wolfe-Quintero K., Inagaki S. & Kim, H. Y. (1998). *Second Language Development in Writing: Measures of Fluency, Accuracy, and Complexity*. Honolulu, HI: Second Language Teaching & Curriculum Center, University of Hawaii.

Yang R. & Allison D. (2003). Research Articles in Applied Linguistics: Moving from Results to Conclusions. *Englsih for Specific Purposes, 33*, 365~385.